ONLY FOOLS & HORSES MISCELLANY

TRIVIA, FACTS & ANECDOTES
FROM THE HIT BBC COMEDY SHOW

ONLY FOOLS & HORSES MISCELLANY

TRIVIA, FACTS & ANECDOTES
FROM THE HIT BBC COMEDY SHOW

PHIL MARTIN

ONLY FOOLS
& HORSES
MISCELLANY

TRIVIA, FACTS & ANECDOTES
FROM THE HIT BBC COMEDY SHOW

© Phil Martin

Phil Martin has asserted his rights in accordance with the Copyright, Designs
and Patents Act 1988 to be identified as the author of this work.

Published By:
Pitch Publishing (Brighton) Ltd
A2 Yeoman Gate
Yeoman Way
Durrington
BN13 3QZ

Email: info@pitchpublishing.co.uk
Web: www.pitchpublishing.co.uk

First published 2008

A catalogue record for this book is available from the British Library.

10-digit ISBN: 1-9054110-5-7
13-digit ISBN: 978-1-9054110-5-4

Printed and bound in Great Britain by Cromwell Press Group

ACKNOWLEDGEMENTS

I'd like to start by thanking scriptwriter John Sullivan and the cast and crew of *Only Fools & Horses* for producing the nation's most-loved comedy series and providing such entertaining and excellent subject matter for this book. Thanks also to Steve Clark, whose *The Only Fools & Horses Story* provided excellent background on the history of the show; and Richard Webber's *The Complete A-Z of Only Fools & Horses*, which was superb for reference and checking facts. Both come highly recommended to any fan of the show. Thanks also to those at Pitch Publishing, for showing belief in the project and for doing an excellent job with the design and layout.

Phil Martin, March 2009

INTRODUCTION

The late, great, British comedy legend Ronnie Barker, once said of *Only Fools & Horses*, "At worst it is excellent, at best brilliant". That wasn't sentiment from Barker for his old pal David Jason, who he starred alongside in *Porridge* and *Open All Hours*. For 22 years, between 1981 and 2003, *Only Fools & Horses* was a national institution in the UK. Christmas specials became part of the British Christmas Day tradition, and there have been some truly unforgettable moments we have all shared with the Trotters.

Everyone has their favourite moments – Del falling through the bar, Grandad's calamity with the chandelier, or Rodney being chased by yobs in the three-wheeled van – but many fans will find it hard to name a favourite episode when asked, because there are just so many good ones to choose from – indeed there has never been a bad episode of the show.

The fact that *Only Fools & Horses* is the nation's favourite comedy is down to a number of different factors, but two very large ones are John Sullivan's supreme skills as a scriptwriter and the cast's ability to bring those scripts to life. David Jason, Nicholas Lyndhurst, Lennard Pearce, Buster Merryfield and all the supporting cast rightly won a place in the nation's heart for their work on *Only Fools & Horses*.

Together, Sullivan and the cast have provided us all with lots of laughs over the years... and plenty of subject matter for this book. I hope readers will enjoy reading this just as much as I enjoyed compiling it, not least because it gave me another excuse to watch all those excellent episodes again and again.

Phil Martin, March 2009

CASTING THE CHARACTERS

The parts of Rodney and Grandad were fairly straightforward casting decisions. BBC head of comedy John Howard Davis decided to cast Nicholas Lyndhurst as Rodney, to which writer John Sullivan and producer Ray Butt were in agreement; Ray Butt sourced Grandad via a trusted agent; but finding the right man to play Derek Trotter proved tricky – and very nearly led to *Only Fools & Horses* grinding to a halt before it had even started. First choice was actor Enn Reitel, but he was tied to Yorkshire Television, filming a series called *Misfits*. Reitel later starred in *The Adventures of Lucky Jim*, before becoming a top voiceover talent working on *Spitting Image* and *X Factor*. Second choice was Jim Broadbent, who Butt went to see in the play *Goosepimples* at the Hampstead Theatre. However Broadbent was tied to the West End production and didn't want to split his time between the new sitcom in the daytime and treading the boards of an evening – although he did later appear as the brilliant detective Roy Slater in future episodes. Billy Murray, who later found fame as DS Beech in *The Bill* and as Johnny Allen in *Eastenders*, was also considered – but on seeing him in the play *Moving*, Butt didn't think Murray fitted the bill. However it wasn't a wasted trip, as he spotted Roger Lloyd-Pack, who would play dippy road sweeper Trigger. Then one night Butt switched on TV and found himself watching an episode of *Open All Hours*. The penny dropped: David Jason, who played shop assistant Granville opposite Ronnie Barker, would be perfect for the role. Sullivan took some convincing – he wondered if Jason had the 'razor sharp edge' required for Del's character – but after hearing the actor read the part he was persuaded and Butt and Sullivan had their Del Boy.

SPOTTED IN BOURNEMOUTH

According to the great man himself, David Jason was discovered at the end of the pier in Bournemouth by Humphrey Barclay. "He cast me as one of the team in *Do Not Adjust Your Set*," explained Jason. "From that I met Ronnie Barker. From Ronnie Barker I met Sid Lotterby and the whole of the [*Only Fools & Horses*] crew; from that I met John Sullivan."

UNION PROBLEMS

The 1991 second part of the two-part Christmas special 'Miami Twice' was filmed on location in Miami – but the fact it was ever made was only due to some hard-nosed negotiations by producer Gareth Gwenlan. He and director Tony Dow had travelled to America prior to filming in preparation for the shoot and the Florida Film Board had assured the pair of them that they would be able to bring their own UK department heads and then hire-in local technicians, make-up artists, wardrobe assistants and others to work beneath them. It was agreed that 60 per cent of the crew would be made up of US-based workers, and the Film Board also assured them that they would be able to hire vans with owner drivers – but it was on this point the project ran into problems. Once in the States, on the first day of filming, the powerful Teamsters Union (which took care of the drivers' interests) had threatened to picket the set and Gwenlan was summoned to a meeting with their boss. "I swear to God, had it not been so serious, I would have thought I was in a bad American B movie. I was shown into this very sombre, dark, wood-panelled office with heavy leather furniture, where I found this great fat, balding guy sitting at his desk." The union boss asked Gwenlan: "What are yous doing in my town?" And the BBC man explained the amount of money being spent and the fact they were employing some sixty local technicians, but the boss wasn't happy and replied, "Yeah, but you ain't employing any of my members." Before telling him to hire at least 12 of his members or face closure. Gwenlan tried to call the Teamsters' bluff and threatened to withdraw, shut down the unit and return to England; that failed with the union boss offering to "drive yous to the airport". Eventually a compromise was reached, with Gwenlan agreeing to employ three Teamsters' drivers; who got paid for doing virtually nothing. One was assigned to drive writer John Sullivan, who later learned his driver had recently been released from prison for armed robbery and murder amongst other crimes. "I gave him a ridiculously big tip because I thought if they had any problems on the set I might have to come back and Charlie would be waiting for me. It was like I gave him a protection money bung!"

CUT TWICE

It is one thing having your only scene cut once from an episode of *Only Fools & Horses,* but actor Michael Bilton suffered the fate twice. His first cut was in 1983. He was cast as a country local in the episode 'Friday the 14th' for a scene in which the boys stop at a pub, on the way down to Boycie's weekend cottage in Cornwall. After Del arrives with the drinks – disappointed that the country boozer doesn't serve Pina Coladas or pizzas – the yokel engages them in conversation and tells them that the weather is on the turn and there will be "a storm of the likes of which you've never seen before". Rodney asks him how he knows; "is it because the cows are all lying down, or can you tell by the clouds?" The yokel replies: "No, I just heard the forecast on Radio 4!" Bilton's second cut came after he was hired to play a guest staying at the Villa Bella guest house the boys check into during the 1989 Christmas special 'The Jolly Boys' Outing'. Arthur (Bilton) and his wife Betty (Fanny Carby) are eating dinner and Del asks them if they're guests or if they have just been hired to cheer the place up. Arthur tells Del that it's horrible, the food's awful, and they're only allowed one jacket potato a day. Del suggests the owner Mrs Creswell might give them an extra lump of custard with their afters... the punch line comes when Arthur explains, "Well she hasn't previous years."

TROTTING INTO LEEDS

During the 2001/02 season the Leeds United player who performed worst in training each week was forced to drive a yellow Reliant Robin, similar to Del Boy's Reliant Regal. Defender Jonathan Woodgate was voted the inaugural 'Plonker of the Week' after the entire Leeds squad had chipped in to buy the old banger as an incentive for players to do well in training. Then-Leeds United chairman Peter Ridsdale said at the time, "I thought it was Trotters Independent Trainers turning up!" Of course, the Trotters themselves were no strangers to driving their three-wheeled motor in Yorkshire: in the episode 'To Hull and Back' Rodney follows Denzil's lorry (with Del locked in the back) all the way to Hull, and along the East Yorkshire coastline.

WHAT'S A YUPPIE?

Del is often getting his French mixed up, and his grasp of English isn't much better either – but perhaps his biggest faux pas is his understanding of the word yuppie. The term yuppie (or yuppy as it is sometimes spelt) means an ambitious young adult, usually college-educated, living in or near a large city, with a professional career and an affluent lifestyle (exactly the life Del aspires to). The word derives from the phrase 'young urban professionals', or less commonly 'young upwardly-mobile professionals' – phrases which were first used in the late 1960s, although the first printed appearance of the word yuppie wasn't until May 1980, in a *Chicago Magazine* article by Dan Rottenberg. However, by the mid-1980s the term had become a derogatory one, but Del doesn't catch on, and is proud to be a yuppie – even though he isn't – leading to the hilarious scene with Cassandra's boss at the bank, Stephen; in which Del tries to convince him he is a yuppie: "You are Stephen take it from me!"

RECORD VIEWING FIGURES

The 'Heroes and Villains' Christmas special in 1996 attracted a United Kingdom record audience of 24.3m – according to BARB, the official body who judge the viewing figures. Diana, Princess of Wales's funeral attracted 31m, but this was a multi-channel event, as was the 25.2m who watched England lose to Germany in the 1990 World Cup Semi Final in Italy. The top ten single-sitting and single-channel audiences are as follows:

Only Fools & Horses (1996) 24.3m
To The Manor Born (1979) 23.9m
Live and Let Die (1980) 23.5m
Jaws (1981) 23.2m
The Spy Who Loved Me (1982) 22.9m
Royal Variety Performance (1967) 22.8m
Diana, Princess of Wales's Panorama interview (1995) 22.75m
Royal Variety Performance (1965) 22.6m
Diamonds are Forever (1981) 22.1m
Crocodile Dundee (1989) 21.7m

BROTHERS DIM

It's there for all to see, but Rodney and Derek are the only ones who actually think they're brothers. "Everyone else thinks they might have different fathers," explains John Sullivan. "They had to be counterparts to each other – one tall, one short, one blond the other dark-haired. They had to look different to each other and at one point when we were casting there was even a suggestion that we had one of them mixed race." Yes, they were both born of the same mother: Joan Mavis Trotter. But did they have the same father? The debate of the brothers' parentage gets touched upon at the end of the first series in 'Christmas Crackers' when the man they both believe to be their father returns. Reg Trotter claims he has a hereditary illness and the boys must have tests, but it's all a trick for him to doctor blood test results and make out Del Boy's a 'whodunnit'. However, Del sees through his lies and sees him off – but not before giving him a bundle of notes to see him alright. Then in the 'Frog's Legacy' the boys learn that Freddy Robdal – a villain from Rotherhithe – has left all his worldly possessions to their mother, including around two million quid's worth of gold bullion. The boys never find it, but in their search for it Del hears rumours that Robdal was having an affair with a married woman on their estate and that she had a son by Robdal. Del's either too daft or his memory of his mother is somewhat different to the reality, and doesn't twig that his brother Rodney is the rumour. Rodney does twig, but reassured by his Uncle Albert that "they're only rumours" the subject isn't mentioned again. That is until writer John Sullivan brilliantly revisits the subject in the last ever episode 'Sleepless in Peckham' – and Rodney learns that, just as he suspected, Robdal was indeed his father.

GRANDAD DEL

When David Jason was asked to attend the casting session for Derek Trotter he had seen the script – but wasn't sure for which role he would be auditioning. Having more than held his own playing the ageing prisoner Blanco in *Porridge*, Jason thought it could be the role of Grandad he was being lined up to play.

GRANDAD'S TEETH

Lennard Pearce, who played Grandad, boasted a complete set of his own teeth. Not much of a problem, apart from when John Sullivan penned episodes in the first and second series which saw the old man losing his false teeth. "Being an old man I assumed Lennard had some false teeth in there, so I wrote one espisode where he didn't have his teeth in. Lennard read it and piped up: 'But I've got all my own teeth!'"

ARTHUR DALEY'S INFLUENCE

John Sullivan believes that ITV's popular series *Minder* played a significant part in *Only Fools & Horses* being commissioned by the BBC. Second-hand car dealer and London-based entrepreneur Arthur Daley (played by George Cole) and his sidekick Terry McCann (Dennis Waterman) were proving so popular in the ratings with their portrayal of urban London that the BBC realised that audiences had an appetite for modern-day London and its wheeler-dealer types. "When *Minder* first came out I was choked because I thought they'd done that modern London," explained Sullivan. "They weren't doing markets or tower blocks but it was modern London and very good and I just thought 'that's the idea gone'. But the BBC changed their minds. I've always given credit to *Minder* for opening that door for me, because without it I don't think that the idea would have ever got used."

FAMOUS FACES

A few famous faces are big fans of the show – including boxer Ricky Hatton, newsreader Sir Trevor McDonald and even the Queen is believed to be a fan. Some have even been lucky enough to make cameo appearances in episodes, as themselves:

Mike Read hosts Top of the Pops in..........It's Only Rock and Roll
Richard Whitmore reads the news in.............. The Sky's the Limit
Richard Branson is seen getting on a plane in........... Miami Twice
Barry Gibb is seen watering his garden in................. Miami Twice
Jonathan Ross hosts Goldrush in .... If They Could See Us Now…!

THE TROTTERS HIT THE SCREENS

On 8th September 1981, the inaugural episode of *Only Fools & Horses* 'Big Brother', which had cost £28,000 to make, was first broadcast on BBC One. The *Radio Times* magazone described the show as the story of 'two brothers living with their grandad in a South London flat and existing off shady deals' – and a total of 9.2 million people tuned in to meet the Trotter family. In that first episode viewers are introduced to Derek, Rodney and their Grandad (whose first name is never revealed in the show, but is actually called Edward Kitchener Trotter). Viewers also learn that Derek and Rodney's mother Joan has died, while dad (who viewers meet in a later episode, and learn is called Reg) deserted the boys not long after their late mother's passing. Derek, Del or Del Boy employs his kid brother despite warnings to the contrary – and although the business is billed as a partnership it's obvious even at this early stage where the balance of power actually lies. Del tells off Rodney for keeping accounts and then for bungling a deal with Trigger, which leaves Trotters Independent Traders with an even bigger bill than originally had been agreed, leaving Del to proclaim, "Today I'd just about clinched a deal to buy these briefcases for £175 when my financial adviser stuck his nose in and advised me to pay £200. And having paid the £200 my financial adviser then advised me to chuck the bleedin' lot in the river. Now with financial advisers like that, who needs a bleedin' recession."

FOREIGN TRAVELS

Viewers join the Trotters on a fair few foreign jaunts over the years. First we see them head off to Benidorm on a package holiday in 'It Never Rains…' after Del cons the local travel agent Alex into offering an 80% discount to the next customer to come into the shop, in a bid to boost his ailing business. Surprise, surprise Del is next through the door and snaps up a bargain holiday to Benidorm, and we see the boys and Grandad off on their travels. Originally it was planned to film this episode in Spain, but BBC budget restraints meant the episode was actually filmed at Studland Bay near Bournemouth in Dorset.

TROTTER FAMILY TREE

In addition to those listed in the family tree, the brothers also have a great uncle Jack Trotter, who according to Albert was a tobacco baron. Their cousins are Stan (married to Jean) and Audrey (married to Kevin). Stan attends Grandad's funeral, with Albert in tow, but leaves him sleeping off a hangover at Nelson Mandela House – and when Del takes Albert back to Stan and Jean's caravan they've hitched up and had it away, leaving Albert living with the brothers! Audrey (or Kevin) doesn't appear in the show, but in the same episode, Albert reveals they sent him off to Sainsburys for some shopping, and when he returned they'd emigrated. It's also worth noting that the brothers' Aunt Ada – who married Albert – had both him and Grandad vying for affections in her younger years. The night they first met Ada, Grandad and Albert ending up brawling in the street outside the local palais, for the affections of a girl Albert tells us looked like Ginger Rogers. Albert separated from Ada and in 'Tea for Three' also reveals that the last time he saw Ada "she looked more like Fred Astaire". Finally, in the episode 'Strangers on the Shore' the boys represent the by then deceased Albert Trotter at a Navy reunion in St Clair La Chapel in France – and it soon becomes apparent that Albert has made more than a few of his own additions to the family tree. One of his Naval colleagues tells Del and Rodney that he had a thing for the local women some fifty-or-so years ago… and most of the local population's fifty-something men are all bald with big white beards!

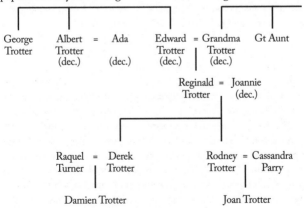

INSPIRATIONS BEHIND DEL BOY

Londoner Chicky Stocker provided John Sullivan with much of the inspiration behind the character of Del. "He was a working-class Londoner and a tough man, but always neatly dressed," explained Sullivan. "He was very genuine and I liked his attitude to life. He was very loyal to his family and I tried to instil that into Del. Other aspects of Del's character, like buying drinks for people down the pub even when he couldn't really afford to, came from people I knew in the car trade. Even if they were doing badly, they'd borrow money to flash about, to let everyone think they were doing well." Another inspiration was Derek Hockley, an old acquaintance of David Jason's. Londoner Hockley ran a building firm who had sub-contracted Jason and his pal Bob Bevil in his days as an electrician. "He had a little goatee beard and was terribly well turned out," explained Jason. "He always had a clean shirt on that was immaculately pressed, a sharp suit, all the jewellery, highly polished shoes and a camel-hair coat – and he just looked the business. He thought he was very smart and what I couldn't get out of my mind was a guy looking as elegantly dressed as he did and yet he spoke like a gorblimey cockney. That really left a great impression on me… He was a great character and, as I got to know him, it became clear that he was a real ducker and diver… I decided to use some of Derek Hockley's attitudes and his dress sense and apply it to Del Boy." Hockley recognised that Jason had taken inspiration from him and wrote to tell him how delighted and proud he was to have provided this inspiration.

CAUGHT ON CAMERA

In one of the early scenes during part two of the Christmas special 'Miami Twice' Del and Rodney ask a passer by to take a photograph of them on a promenade in Miami. The passer by has a compact camera hanging around his neck – but preferring Del's more-upmarket model runs off as the brothers are striking a pose for the snap. All we see is Del giving chase and Rodney's expression of exasperation, but in the next scene Del Boy walks into the office from which they're about to pick up their camper van with both his own camera and the American thief's compact around his neck.

SIR DAVID

When Sir David Jason was knighted in 2005, he admitted he was humbled when receiving his honour from Her Majesty the Queen. He said at the time, "The Queen said 'you've been in the business a long time'. I said I hope I hadn't offended her at any time and she said she didn't think so." Asked how Del Boy would have reacted, Sir David said, "He would have said, 'Stone me Rodders, we'll have to come back tonight, she's got some good gear here.'" On the day he collected his knighthood, Jason also publicly revealed that he had married long-term partner Gill Hinchcliffe in a secret ceremony. The couple, who have a daughter Sophie Mae, wed in front of family and friends at the Dorchester Hotel in London.

READIES

The original working title for *Only Fools & Horses* was *Readies* – but writer John Sullivan wasn't happy with this, as far as he was concerned this was only a working title. Sullivan explained, "I always thought longer titles grabbed people's eyes and obviously I wanted to make viewers aware of us. I like the idea of calling the show *Only Fools & Horses* from the old expression 'only fools and horses work', because Del's main aim in life is not to work and yet he scurries around till eleven at night working his socks off not to work." The expression Sullivan had coined the title from was an old American slang saying, which had worked its way across the Atlantic, and back in the early 1980s not everyone had heard it. The BBC took some convincing. They were also considering other titles including 'Big Brother' (which was eventually the title for the opening episode) – but after weeks of haggling Sullivan persuaded the bosses his title was right for the show.

SUBTITLED

Subtitles appear in just one episode of *Only Fools & Horses*. It is during the first series, in 'Cash and Curry' when Mr Ram speaks Indian to tell a curry house waiter: "If this idiot asks for anything else, tell him the kitchen is closed."

RODNEY'S FETISH

It's during the first series, in the second episode 'Go West Young Man' to be precise, that Del first learns of his brother's fetish for girls in uniform and – much to his older brother's disgust – that Rodney's favourite is a policewoman. Sat in a Soho nightclub Rodney confesses to Del that the reason he is having relationship problems with his girlfriend Monica is down to his uniform fetish and his attempts to get her to dress as a policewoman. Rodney's fetish also rears its head in 'Long Legs of the Law' when his dreams eventually come true and he actually takes a pretty WPC by the name of Sandra out on a date to the cinema – but the blossoming relationship is doomed the moment Rodney invites her back to the flat and she recognises much of the brothers' possessions as nicked. She ends the fledgling relationship and then gives Rodney 24 hours' grace to get rid of all the hookey gear.

RUNNER UP TO MAN ON THE MOON

According to readers of *Radio Times* magazine, only man landing on the moon rates as a greater television moment than Del Boy falling through the bar in the episode 'Yuppy Love'. The survey was conducted by the magazine in 1999, and it asked readers to vote across three categories: factual, drama and comedy. In third place was the Daleks saying "Exterminate!" in *Dr Who*.

JOHN'S BIGGEST INFLUENCE

According to the man himself, John Sullivan's biggest influence on his writing was his father. "He was a prisoner of war, a bookies' runner and an illegal boxer – and he had some great stories." A keen card player, it's easy to see his father's influence in the episode 'A Losing Streak'. Del appears to be having a dreadful run of luck – but we learn Boycie's cheating with a marked deck. But Del outfoxes him with a clever switch around of his own cards to give him an almost unbeatable hand. But perhaps the biggest influence from John Sullivan senior comes in 'A Touch of Glass' – the famous episode with the chandelier scene. Sullivan senior had been working at a mansion when the same thing happened...

LICENSED TO DRIVE?

In the second episode John Sullivan wrote for Rodney to drive a battered old Ford Cortina GT – cadged by Del from Boycie's car lot – back to Nelson Mandela House. The brakes are a bit spongy and Rodney comes flying around the corner and nearly runs his brother down. A hilarious scene, but watching it you wouldn't realise Nicholas Lyndhurst didn't have a driving licence at the time. "Technically we weren't on a public road where we filmed it, but even so I told Nick not to go too fast," explained experienced BBC producer Ray Butt, who had an old camera trick up his sleeve to give the scene comic value. "I was going to under-crank the film – which meant it would come out looking like it had been speeded up. He came round the corner and it looked unbelievable. The tyres were screaming and black smoke was pouring out the back because we'd put smoke canisters under it… He did it even faster than I'd asked him. Even though Nick hadn't passed his test he was still a superb driver."

MIND THE GAP

There is a 13-year age gap between brothers Derek and Rodney, which is something viewers learn in the very first episode of *Only Fools & Horses*: "You couldn't be like any other little brother could you eh? And come along a couple of years later after me. Oh no, no, not you," explains Del Boy. "You had to wait 13 years. So while all the other mods were having punch-ups down at Southend and going to The Who concerts I was at home babysitting. I could never get your oyster milk stains out me Ben Shermans… I used to find Rusks in me Hush Puppies!"

WHAT'S IN A NAME?

How John Sullivan named a number of venues in the scripts was influenced by his own life. The (Down by the) Riverside Club was named after an amateur football team he'd come across, while the Dockside Secondary Modern School was actually named after his father's school, while the influence for the casino the One Eleven Club was the fact that Sullivan lived at house number 111!

BIOGRAPHY: JOHN SULLIVAN

John grew up in post-war London. Born in 1946 he grew up in
Balham in South London; his father John senior was a plumber, while
mother Hilda occasionally took work as a charlady - but for most of
his childhood, she was a housewife. A keen football follower, John took
little interest in schoolwork, apart from English classes. Having failed his
eleven-plus in 1957, he left school at 15 years of age, and took work as a
messenger with news agency Reuters and later with ad agency Collett,
Dickinson and Pearce. Next it was cleaning cars in the second-hand
motor trade - probably where most of Boycie's influences were spotted
- before working for Watney's delivering and stacking crates of beer. It
was during this time John first tried his hand at scriptwriting, along with
his work-mate Paul Saunders; it was rejected by the BBC. Undeterred,
John continued to write scripts and sent off various treatments. After
following in his father's footsteps and working in the plumbing trade,
which didn't go well, John eventually decided he needed a job with the
BBC to get his scripts under the noses of the men who mattered. He
landed a role in the props department and from there moved on to
work as a scene shifter. With what he believed to be a killer script, for
the series *Citizen Smith*, up his sleeve John eventually plucked up the
courage to approach producer Dennis Main-Wilson in the BBC bar
to push his idea forward. "Twice I started walking across to him and
both times I bottled it. The third time he spotted me. Our eyes met and
I had no choice but to actually go over and introduce myself." Fearing
the sack, John said, "Dennis, I'm John Sullivan. I thought I'd introduce
myself because we're going to be working together soon." Charmed by
his brazen wit, Main-Wilson gave John plenty of advice - the main
piece being for him to go away and write sketches for *The Dave Allen
Show* or *The Two Ronnies*. He approached Ronnie Barker, while working
on the set of *Porridge*, and was told to bring in his sketch ideas; they
impressed Barker so much that he was put on a contract to write for the
show. That in turn impressed Main-Wilson, who then told John to go
off and write *Citizen Smith*. Taking two weeks' leave, he spent the time
encamped in the home of girlfriend Sharon's parents in Crystal Palace
and then delivered the finished article to Main-Wilson. He loved it, so
too did Jimmy Gilbert the BBC's Head of Light Entertainment. The
pilot was made and in 1977 it was screened as part of *Comedy Special*, an

anthology of one-off comedy shows, and it fared very well, so much so that the first series was commissioned shortly afterwards and John quit his job as a scene shifter. From there he moved onto *Only Fools & Horses*, and since then he has also scripted the following shows:

Just Good Friends.. BBC, 1983-86
Dear John .... BBC, 1986-87
Sitting Pretty .... BBC, 1992-93
With Over Here..BBC, 1996
Roger, Roger... BBC 1996-2003
Heartburn Hotel .... BBC, 1998-2000
Micawber..ITV, 2001-02

BERNI INN

Derek's idea of impressing a lady is taking her for a steak meal at a Berni Inn: one of the UK's original pub chains founded in the 1950s by Aldo Berni. When he joins a computer dating agency, through which he meets Raquel, he tells the clerk, "You can tell the lucky lady she is guaranteed a steak meal!" However his love of Berni Inns surfaces long before this point, in 'Go West Young Man'. After meeting stunners Nicky and Michelle in a nightclub he tells Rodney that "we'll take 'em to a Berni Inn," thinking they'll be impressed. Later, in 'Yesterday Never Comes', he takes "posh tart" Miranda Davenport to one. We don't actually see them dining, but we know they've been because when Del returns to the flat he tells Miranda what a blinding meal it was, to which she replies: "Yes, it was very nice. I did feel a bit overdressed for a Berni Inn though." The first Berni Inn opened in Bristol in 1955, it was bought out by Whitbread, who phased out the Berni Inn name in favour of their own Beefeaters or Brewers Fayre brand.

MIKE'S WISH

Ken McDonald, who played Nag's Head landlord Mike Fisher, sadly died in August 2001 – but it was always his wish that he should remain in the show. So in the most-recent trilogy (2001-2003), Sid is running the pub, while the character of Mike Fisher is in prison for embezzlement.

TOP SITCOM VOTE

In March 2004, the public voted *Only Fools & Horses* the top television sitcom of all time. The results of the poll were revealed on a live BBC show fronted by Jonathan Ross. (Ross appeared in the show: a cameo role playing himself, in the 2001 episode 'If They Could See Us Now...!')

Only Fools & Horses	(22.2%)
Blackadder	(18.3%)
Vicar of Dibley	(13.8%)
Dad's Army	(11.3%)
Fawlty Towers	(11.2%)
Yes Minister	(8%)
Porridge	(6.1%)
Open All Hours	(4.4%)
The Good Life	(2.6%)
One Foot in the Grave	(2%)

The public were first asked to choose their favourite sitcoms from a list of one hundred. The final ten were then championed by celebrity fans. More than one and a half million votes were received for all ten of the different comedy shows, and with 342,426 votes *Only Fools & Horses* gained 22.2% - which was championed by TV presenter David Dickinson. David Jason said of the result, "I am delighted that something which gave me some of the happiest times of my life still gives pleasure to so many people." Writer John Sullivan added, "I started writing *Only Fools & Horses* in 1981 because I knew that in 23 years' time there would be a Britain's Best Sitcom competition and I wanted to win it. I'm delighted for everyone connected with the series and my thanks to everyone who voted for us."

DID YOU KNOW?

'Only Fools & Horses' was the title of a 1979 episode of *Citizen Smith*, also penned by *Only Fools & Horses* writer John Sullivan, starring *Steptoe and Son* star Wilfred Brambell.

SCIENTISTS VOTE

In December 2004, scientists deemed *Only Fools & Horses* the funniest comedy ever. Various factors were considered by the scientist Dr Helen Pilcher and writer Timandra Harkness, who carried out the research on behalf of the TV channel UK Gold. These included the qualities of the main character and their delusions of grandeur; the verbal wit of the script; social status between the sitcom's highest and lowest ranking characters; and the number of times somebody fell over. Dr Pilcher, of the Comedy Research Project, explained, "This formula shows why some sitcoms fail to make the grade whilst others are destined to make us laugh time and time again." *Only Fools & Horses* scored 696 in the formula, while in second place BBC comedy *The Office*, written by Ricky Gervais and Stephen Merchant, got 678 and Channel 4's *Father Ted* finished in third position with a score of 564.

CHRISTMAS CRACKERS

Four of the Trotters' Christmas escapades made it into a poll to find the top ten best Christmas TV shows in 2002. Christmas shoppers across Britain were polled and top of the pile was the 1996 Christmas special 'Heroes & Villians', famous for Del Boy and Rodney dressing up as Batman and Robin. That was followed by the episode 'Miami Twice', which sees Del used as a ringer for a drug lord by a Miami mafia family. In seventh place is the 1989 episode 'The Jolly Boys' Outing', and 1985's 'To Hull and Back' was ninth.

THE DESERT INN

In the episode 'Stage Fright', Starlight Rooms compere Eric claims that Raquel and Tony (the singing dustman) had just finished a sell-out season at The Desert Inn, Las Vegas. This is absolute rubbish, fed to him by Del, but in truth The Desert Inn was a world famous hotel, casino and golf course in Nevada which operated from 1950 to the year 2000. It was the fifth resort to open on the Las Vegas Strip; locals nicknamed it 'DI'. It was where the first *Ocean's Eleven* was shot in 1960 and was regularly used for TV and films, with the last film shot there being *Rush Hour 2*.

SERIES VIEWING FIGURES

Series One 7.7m

Series Two 8.8m

Series Three 10.5m

Series Four.. 14.9m

Series Five... 16m

Series Six 16.7m

Series Seven.. 16.8m

Christmas Specials

Christmas Crackers – 1981 .... 7.5m

Christmas Trees – 1982 .... 7.2m

Diamonds are for Heather – 1982............................ 9.3m

Thicker Than Water – 1983 .... 10.8m

To Hull and Back – 1985 .... 16.9m

A Royal Flush – 1986.. 18.8m

The Frog's Legacy – 1987 .... 14.5m

Dates – 1988 .... 16.6m

The Jolly Boys' Outing – 1989 .... 20.1m

Rodney Come Home – 1990.................................... 18m

Miami Twice Part One – 1991 .... 17.7m

Miami Twice Part Two – 1991 .... 14.9m

Mother Nature's Son – 1992 .... 20.1m

Fatal Extraction – 1993 .... 19.6m

Heroes and Villains – 1996 .... 21.3m

Modern Men – 1996 .... 21.3m

Time On Our Hands – 1996 .... 24.3m

If They Could See Us Now…! – 2001 .... 20.3m

Strangers on the Shore – 2002 .... 16.3m

Sleepless in Peckham – 2003 .... 15.5m

THE MIAMI TRIGGER

With Trigger back in England, in 'Miami Twice' Del and Rodney bump into Rico and the rest of the 'family' in Miami including Lurch – who seems to be the US version of Trigger. The dozy Italian-American does, however, manage to call Rodney by the name on his birth certificate.

WORLDWIDE APPEAL

Only Fools & Horses has not just enjoyed continued success in the UK, the BBC has sold the show all across the world, with a new audio track being dubbed in the native language where necessary. It's been aired in Australia, Barbados, Belgium, Croatia, Cyprus, Greece, Hong Kong, Ireland, Malta, New Zealand, Pakistan, Poland, South Africa and Spain, amongst others. While in the Netherlands the rights to the show were sold and the scripts translated into the programme *Wat Schuift't?* (What's It Worth), with the characters rechristened Stef (Del), Robbie (Rodney) and Granpa (Grandad). There has also been a Portuguese remake, while the Americans have deliberated over the idea of remaking *Only Fools & Horses* – replacing the Trotters with an Irish family – but it is yet to come to fruition.

KEEPING ACCOUNTS

Del Boy never kept accounts for several reasons, too much paperwork for one, evidence for the tax man another. And Del was furious with his younger brother when he caught him keeping accounts in the very first episode: "You're keeping accounts now," says Del. "Well there you are, Grandad. A lot of people told me I was a right dipstick to make my brother a partner in the business but this only goes to prove how bloody right they were. You dozy little twonk, Rodney. This is prima facie evidence. If the tax man gets hold of that he'll put us away for three years." Lucky for Del that Rodney did keep those early records, as in 1996 when the Lesser Watch is found, those old records include a receipt for the house clearance which included the timepiece and enabled the boys to prove it was legally theirs.

RODNEY'S WEDDING

"He looked like Peter Crouch with a top hat on!" That was how Patrick Murray, who played Rodney's dopey pal Mickey Pearce, described how Rodney Charlton Trotter looked in his top hat and tails for his on-screen wedding to Cassandra Louise Parry, during the episode 'Little Problems'.

RICKY'S UNUSUAL WARM UP

In September 2004, BBC Sport reported that boxer Ricky Hatton could be seen cruising the streets of Hyde in a replica of Del Boy's three-wheeled van. The Manchester fighter said, "I have been a huge fan of *Only Fools & Horses* for as long as I can remember. It's the best programme on TV. When I was barely into my teens I told my dad that one day I'd have one of the three-wheelers from the series and he looked at me as if I was mad. He laughed it off... but now I've made it come true. I couldn't be happier." Hatton bought the van complete with Trotters Independent Trading logo from the *Only Fools & Horses* Appreciation Society, and also snapped up a Del Boy's trademark sheepskin coat and flat cap, and completed the look with a fake cigar.

DEL'S ON THE DREAM LISTING

As part of their 80th anniversary celebrations in 2004, *Radio Times* asked its readers to nominate their dream evening line-up of television programmes and times, and the result was as follows:

7.00pm	The Simpsons
7.30pm	EastEnders
8.00pm	Who Wants to be a Millionaire?
8.30pm	Only Fools & Horses
9.00pm	Casualty
9.30pm	A Touch of Frost
10.00pm	News
10.30pm	Movie première

THREE WHEELER VANDALS

In July 2003 yobs vandalised Del Boy's three-wheeled van. The BBC used three different versions of the Reliant Regal, and it was one of these which was on display at a festival in Cornwall. The offenders scaled a security fence surrounding the National Film Exhibition in St Agnes and smashed the windscreen causing £100 worth of damage. Whether Boyce's garage conducted the repairs is unknown, but the Driscoll brothers might be on the lookout for the offenders!

WHO WANTS TO BE A MILLIONAIRE

The 2001 Christmas special 'If They Could See Us Now...!' had originally been scripted to see Del Boy on the quiz show *Who Wants To Be A Millionaire?* However, the BBC could not reach an agreement with ITV over a deal to allow one of their flagship shows to be used within *Only Fools & Horses*. ITV demanded the right to show a repeat of the episode, but the BBC would not allow licence-fee payers' money to be used to fund the actors' repeat episode fees, to enable the show to be screened on ITV. John Sullivan was left with no choice but to rewrite the show and instead he created a one-off show, similar to the ITV quiz, called *Goldrush*. This was hosted by BBC presenter Jonathan Ross, who appeared in a cameo role as himself. Writer John Sullivan said at the time he had originally hoped the two broadcasters could put aside their differences for the one-off special. "Like the British and German armies playing football on Christmas Day in the First World War, it would have been fantastic to put the ratings war aside for one day."

A WENDY

A 'Wendy' was how the cast and crew of *Only Fools & Horses* described the gags which caused the biggest laughs during the show – recorded in front of a live audience. John Challis, who played Boycie, explained, "The biggest laugh ever in the history of *Only Fools & Horses* was reckoned to be a line that Grandad said very early on." And that line came after the following exchange between Del and Rodney, about Rodney's new business with Mickey Pearce.

Rod: We're going into the self catering holiday trade.
Del: What on two hundred nicker?
Rod: Yeah, well we're starting in a small way
Grandad: What you got… a wendy house?

Patrick Murray, who played Mickey Pearce, explained, "After that whenever we had the read through [the script] and we came across a really funny line you would hear someone saying, 'Well there's another Wendy'."

GENTLEMEN

John Sullivan's first comedy script was co-written with Watney's work buddy Paul Saunders and called *Gentlemen*. The two had gone to school together, and ended up working together, stacking crates amongst other things, at the brewery. "He was a funny guy with a dry wit," explained Sullivan. After reading an article about *Til Death Us Do Part* writer Johnny Speight, Paul told his pal, "We're pretty funny guys. We could do this." They did: bashing out a script on a two-quid typewriter. It was about a man who ran an old-fashioned gents' convenience, with brass pipes and china troughs - but started losing customers to a new toilet down the road. Sullivan admitted it was awful and unsurprisingly the BBC rejected it, saying it wasn't the type of material they were looking to commission. Further solo efforts, about a family called the Leeches and another about a football team, were also rejected before Sullivan hit the target with *Citizen Smith*.

THIRD TIME LUCKY

Del and Rodney miss out on becoming a millionaire on two separate occasions over the years – before they finally hit the jackpot in 1996. In 1987 they miss out on when they can't find Freddie the Frog's hidden stash of gold bullion, left to them by their late mother and worth over a million quid. Two years later, during the "Groovy Gang" episode, Rodney wins the Spanish State Lottery but cannot claim the million peseta prize because his passport says he's under the age of 18. Finally it's third time lucky when Raquel's dad spots the missing Harrison Lesser Watch amongst their stock – and it is sold at Sotheby's for £6.2m.

OTHER LANGUAGES

In 'Miami Twice' both Del and Rodney struggle with some of Rico's American dialogue and vice versa. Both are confused when he tells them the local police force 'don't know their ass from first base'. While Rico's brief Salvatore has to explain some of the English phrases used by Del, but most of them are even beyond the lawyer.

SPECIAL EPISODES

There have been five special episodes of *Only Fools & Horses*, which weren't part of the regular series and Christmas specials. 'Christmas Trees' an eight-minute episode was broadcast in 1982 during *The Funny Side Of Christmas*, a variety show hosted by Frank Muir and including mini episodes of *Yes Minister, Open All Hours, Butterflies* and *Last Of The Summer Wine*. 'Licensed To Drill' is a an educational episode, made in 1984 but never aired on domestic television, and only shown in schools. On Christmas Eve 1985, Del appeared in a BBC *Breakfast Time* spoof documentary in which reporter and consumer champion Lynn Faulds Wood investigates his claims that the white mice he's selling would turn into horses at midnight. 'The Robin Flies At Dawn' was a special episode filmed for British troops fighting in the 1991 Gulf War, with a morale-boosting good-luck message. Finally, in 1997 Del, Rodney and Albert filmed a Comic Relief Special appealing for donations to the BBC charity.

DETECTIVE CASSANDRA

In 1997 Gwyneth Strong, who played Cassandra, also appeared alongside David Jason in an episode of ITV's detective drama *A Touch of Frost*. Playing the role of DS Bailey – Jason's character DI Jack Frost's boss – there's a wonderful double entendre when she first appears in the episode and reminds Frost they've met before.

THE BEST COMES TO THOSE WHO WAIT

It's been voted the funniest comedy clip in British TV history, but for the scene in which Del Boy falls through the open bar in the bistro John Sullivan actually had to wait a decade or so to use the gag. Years earlier Sullivan told David Jason he had actually seen it happen and would love to use it in the show – but didn't know how or where to incorporate it into the script. "We waited ten years to use it," revealed Sullivan. The scene was shot in one take as Jason carried off the fall in style, before emerging to tell a confused Trigger, who's completely unaware of what's gone on, "Drink up Trig... drink up we're leaving."

BIOGRAPHY: DAVID JASON

Sir David Jason OBE was born during the Second World War as one of twin brothers and christened David White; he took the stage name David Jason, by combining his first name with the name of his twin brother who sadly died at birth. He was born on 2nd February 1940, in Edmonton, London and brought up in Lodge Lane, North Finchley, by parents Arthur (a porter at Billingsgate Fish Market) and Olwyn (a cleaner) and went to school nearby. On leaving school he trained as an electrician and combined his work as a sparky around London with part-time theatre work; he broke into television by playing the role of Bert Bradshaw in the television show *Crossroads* in 1964. In 1967 he became part of the *Do Not Adjust Your Set* team, a BBC comedy show featuring various sketches, where he worked alongside Eric Idle, Terry Jones and Michael Palin. David Jason was recruited to the show to offset the rather intellectual style of Idle, Jones and Palin with his masterly sense of timing. His performances caught the attention of Ronnie Barker, who was soon to become a mentor to Jason. In 1969 Jason was recruited to appear in *Hark At Barker* and in 1973 he appeared alongside Barker as Granville in a pilot episode of *Open All Hours*, and between 1976 and 1985 four series of the show were made. He also featured in Barker's *Porridge*, a prison-based comedy, as ageing con Blanco. In 1981 he was cast as Derek Trotter in *Only Fools & Horses*, the role for which he is best remembered. But it isn't just his comedy for which Jason is widely admired. His dramatic work, including *The Darling Buds of May* and as detective chief inspector Jack Frost in *A Touch of Frost*, has also won him plaudits. In addition to his acting roles he has also worked on radio and as a voice artist on a number of children's television productions, providing voices for *Danger Mouse, The BFG, Count Duckula* and Toad from *The Wind in the Willows*. In 1993, David Jason was awarded an OBE; in 2005 he made the Queen's Birthday Honours List, and was knighted for services to acting. Away from the screen Jason is a devoted family man. His long-time partner Myfanwy Talog sadly died in 1995 after a long battle with breast cancer. He subsequently met Gill Hinchcliffe whom he married in a secret ceremony at the Dorchester Hotel in London on 30 November 2005. The couple have a daughter Sophie Mae who was born in 2001. His career record is listed on the next page.

Television

Films

Animation

THAT'S A LOVELY LOOKING CORK

Del loves to think he's at home in any walk of life – "drinking lager at the Nag's Head or sipping Pimms at Henley Regatta" - but in 'Miami Twice' Rodney has to tell him he's supposed to test the bouquet of the wine when the waiter hands him the cork, which Del does... by sucking the end! He then tells the waiter "Pour on McDuff". The correct saying is actually 'Lead on McDuff' which originated from the line 'Lay on Macduff' in the final scene of Shakespeare's *Macbeth*.

DIPPY DEL'S ETHNIC TOURS

In the episode 'Slow Bus To Chingford' Del launches his Ethnic Tours and promises a tour of London which the best tour guide in the city would fail to deliver! He tells Rodney he'll take sightseers to see:

The house where Sherlock Holmes was born
The summit of Mount Pleasant
Where Jack the Ripper was buried

Del also tells Rod he will tell them how the Elephant & Castle got its name with a yarn about Richard the Lionheart having a castle about where the roundabout is located and that Hannibal and his elephants lay siege to the castle. In truth the Elephant & Castle (which is a major London road junction) got its name from a pub of the same name which was located at the junction; while Del's story doesn't quite work, as Hannibal led his elephants across the Alps (and nowhere near South London) in 218; while Richard the Lionheart wasn't born until nearly a thousand years later.

OPENING CREDITS

The opening credits of *Only Fools & Horses* features a number of snapshots of 1980s London, but the actual tower block which appears as Nelson Mandela House is Harlech Tower, Park Road East, Acton. That was also used for filming in the first few series of the show, but from 1988 Whitemead House in Bristol was used after the show moved out of London.

FOOTBALL ALLEGIANCE

Rodney is undoubtedly a Chelsea fan – but quite who Derek supports is open for debate. Rodney's allegiance to the Blues is revealed when Del Boy tells his brother: "The sky's blue and Chelsea are going to win the cup." Rodney's support of Chelsea also crops up at the posh dinner in the 1986 Christmas special 'A Royal Flush' when his girlfriend Vicky reveals, "Rodney's going to take me to a soccer match next week". The game in question is at Stamford Bridge, home of Chelsea, and Rodney admits to being a regular in the Shed. With the conversation on Chelsea circa 1986, and in particular one of the team's stars of that era Kerry Dixon, Derek interrupts to proclaim, "They should never have sold Greavsie". In typical irrelevant fashion, Del is referring to the long-time retired Jimmy Greaves, who had left Chelsea for AC Milan in 1960. Del Boy's favourite team is less obvious. In the first ever episode a Crystal Palace scarf is seen hanging with the coats in the Trotter's porch – but this could of course belong to Grandad or even be a piece of stock! Also in series one, during 'Slow Bus to Chingford', Rodney refers to his brother as the "cultural advisor to the Chelsea Shed". Del could of course follow one if not both of the teams supported by his parents. Reg Trotter can be assumed to be a Millwall fan. Grandad tells Rodney, "Your dad always said that one day Del Boy would reach the top… then again he used to say that one day Millwall would win the cup!" Del Boy's fondness for Millwall is obvious in 'Rodney Come Home'. When disappointed that Albert is no help in coming up with an idea to persuade Rodney not to take Tania to the pictures he exclaims: "I was hoping you might be able to help… but then again I was hoping that Millwall would win the UEFA Cup!" Their mother's team comes to light in 'Little Problems' when Rodney's middle name is revealed as Charlton. "My mum was a fan," explains Del Boy, to which Marlene enquires, "What Charlton Heston?" Del retorts, "No… Charlton Athletic!"

LOVELY JUBBLY

Del is often heard to utter the phrase "Lovely Jubbly" when things are going well. It means excellent or great, and originally came from a 1950s' advertisement for an ice lolly, by the name of Jubbly.

ALBERT'S MINICAB

A cracking visual gag during the 1987 Christmas special 'The Frog's Legacy' was seeing Rodney dressed as a chief mourner, leading a funeral cortège through the streets of Peckham (although the scene was actually shot in Colchester, Essex). The sight of the hearse pulling into view also sets up Boycie to proclaim: "Albert, your minicab's arrived!" Ray Butt explained this joke was something he had picked up in his local boozer. "We used to go to a local pub called the Duke of York; this pub was right opposite an undertaker's shop; and one day we were in there and the boys who had just done a funeral came right in – they had all their black gear on. As they came through the door a bloke shouted out, 'Oi Tom, your minicab's arrived!' A few months later that actually turned up in the script."

IT'S ARTHUR'S ASHES

"It's Arthur's Ashes," exclaims Rodney on opening the urn Del's bought as part of Trigger's grandmother's house clearance. "Ain't that the black bloke who won Wimbledon?" asks Del Boy.

DEL'S POEM

After flogging a second-hand banger in 'Go West Young Man' to an Australian for near on two hundred nicker, Del's moved to recite a little poem. He leaves us guessing on the final word off his ditty...

As I was walking through Earl's Court
Into a pub I was lured
Where a nosy pom
said where you from
As I downed the amber fluid
I said get straight
I'm an Aussie mate
And I'm fixing to get plastered
But the beer is crook
and the birds all look
like you, you pommy...

LONDON TO BRISTOL

Such is the show's popularity, particularly in the nation's capital, in 1988 the BBC had to move filming away from London to Bristol - which also coincided with the change in format to 50-minute episodes. As the show's stock rose during the 1980s, the more difficult it became for the crew to film in London, as fans would flock to catch a glimpse of their favourite show being shot. Added to that the London markets were difficult to use, because the traders didn't like the disruption! Bristol was suggested as a new 'home' for the Trotters, and after Tony Dow and John Sullivan went on a recce mission it was decided the city had everything required to film: the pubs, houses, a market and a tower block - and to give Bristol a more London feel, the Beeb would take their own red London buses to use in the background during filming.

HOBSON'S CHOICE

John Sullivan was never afraid of using a choice slang phrase in his scripts, for example when the coach party are stranded on 'The Jolly Boys' Outing' to Margate, when Alan Parry (Cassandra's dad) says, "What we've got here is Hobson's choice." This actually means there is only one option to choose: meaning the choice is therefore between taking the option or not. The phrase is said to originate from Thomas Hobson a livery stable owner in Cambridge who, in order to rotate the use of his horses, offered customers the choice of either taking the horse in the stall nearest the door – or taking none at all.

UNCLE'S SECRET

When Cassandra loses her baby in the episode 'Modern Men' it's in a scene which was eventually cut from the final edit that Albert reveals that he too suffered the same cruel blow when he was married to the boys' aunt Ada. Del asks him why he had never mentioned it before and if it was the stress of the miscarriage which caused his break up with Ada, to which Albert responds, "No, son. But it would have if she'd found out about it!" He goes onto explain that it was "some woman I met in Honolulu".

DEL'S TV APPEARANCES

Across the seven series and Christmas specials, Del Boy makes three appearances on television during *Only Fools & Horses*.

Number 1: In 'The Miracle of Peckham' he is interviewed by an American TV news station which has come to the church to film the supposed miracle, which Del has discovered. The interview is abruptly ended by Father O'Keith – who's just discovered there is no miracle and that a leaky roof is why the statue of the Virgin Mary is weeping.

Number 2: In the feature-length 'Miami Twice', Del and Rodney are filmed leaving the villa of Vincenzo Occhetti by another American TV news crew who incorrectly assume Del Boy is the Mafia Don to whom he bears a striking resemblance. The pictures also make it onto the BBC news and Raquel, Albert, Mickey Pearce, Denzil, Sid and Mike all see it on the TV in the Nag's Head. Del (being mistaken for Occhetti) is described as 'Public Enemy Number One' to which Raquel exasperates: "But he only left on Tuesday."

Number 3: Another TV appearance for Del comes in 'If They Could See Us Now' on the spoof BBC quiz show *Goldrush*, hosted by Jonathan Ross (who makes a cameo appearance as himself). The show is specially created for the episode, although writer John Sullivan had wanted Del to appear on *Who Wants to be a Millionaire*. However, the request was rebuffed, meaning Sullivan had to come up with a BBC version.

Meanwhile, the boy's exploits also make the TV news on three separate occasions. Firstly during the episode 'Danger UXD' the local news reporting the theft of the inflatable dolls from the back of Denzil's van: Denzil's watching the news in a Chinese takeaway, when news of their theft is announced on the local news after a forged signature (Del Boy's) was discovered on the delivery docket. Then in 'The Sky's The Limit' Del mistakenly buys a satellite dish from Bronco – believing it to be Boycie's missing receiver – but at the end of the show Del and Rodney discover it's actually the one that the news is reporting nicked from Heathrow airport, causing chaos and leading to flights being cancelled or re-routed – including Cassandra's flight home from holiday. Finally in 'Mother Nature's Son' it's the drums of luminous chemicals cleared from the Trotter allotment and dumped in a pond by Denzil and Trigger, unbeknown to Rodney, which hit the headlines. The chemical pollutes the water supply and the news reports the London Borough of Peckham is without water.

LAST EPISODE?

'Who Wants To Be A Millionaire' was originally written as a final episode of *Only Fools & Horses*. It came at the end of the fifth series and John Sullivan wrote it after David Jason had told him over dinner that he felt five series was enough, and that the show had run its course. The series finale would end with Del taking up the offer to jet off to Australia and team up in business with his old school pal Jumbo Mills, leaving Rodney behind, because his immigration application is turned down due to his drugs conviction. "The last scene was to have seen Del flying out of the country and Rodney walking out of the airport looking a bit lost," explained Sullivan. The BBC planned to continue the series under a new title *Hot Rod* with Jason having the option to return at a later date. However, a change of heart meant Jason was on board for a sixth series, which also saw the shows change to the new 50-minute format.

DOUBLE TAKE

In 'Miami Twice' David Jason plays his usual character of Del but also Del's look-a-like: Mafia Don Vincent Occhetti, who is trying to bump him off, but only English-born actor Nick Stringer can claim to have played two different characters in two different episodes. He first appears in the second episode of the first series as the Australian who buys an old banger from Del and then runs into the back of Boycie's E-type Jaguar. He appears again in the sixth episode of series five, as Del's old mate Jumbo Mills, who'd emigrated to Australia but is back in England to set up his new car import business. He offers Del Boy and Rodney jobs, but after Rodney's visa application is rejected, Del stays in the UK. In addition to various other roles, including *The Sweeney* and *Coronation Street*, Stringer also appeared with Nicholas Lyndhurst in *Goodnight Sweetheart*.

HEARD AND NOT SEEN

Several memorable characters are heard of, but never actually seen. Mickey Pearce and Marlene Boyce started out this way, but were written into the script as characters by John Sullivan. However, here are a few who never actually made it onto screen:

Bend Over Benson: Del, Trigger, Boycie and Denzil's old headmaster at the Martin Luther King Comprehensive. It's unlikely he would ever be seen as he's locked up and doctors recommended he never be released back into society, but if he did appear he would have been easy to spot, as he has a scar running down from the bridge of his nose and his right ear is missing.

Alfie Flowers: He tucks up Del with some broken lawnmower engines when he's bit non-compos-mentis down the One Eleven Club; Del shifts them to Rodney, who's broken away to form a partnership with Mickey Pearce.

Paddy the Greek: A regular contact of Del's, first heard of when Rodney buys a blue serge suit from him for his bird Monica. Del buys lead off him in 'The Miracle of Peckham' but discovers it's nicked from the church roof; Paddy also flogs Rodney the white sports jacket and tie he wears in 'Watching the Girls Go By' and is the source of nine-carat goal identity bracelets Del is flogging in 'Heroes and Villians'. He also gives Rodney one, inscribed Rooney, and tries to convince him it's 24-carat gold.

Monkey Harris: A regular business contact of Del's and an old pal from his schooldays: they both played for the Dockside Secondary Modern school football team – Monkey played left-back, Del Boy in midfield. He's first heard of in the episode 'Long Legs of the Law' as Del tells Grandad about a fight he had with business partner Tommy Razzle. Del explains that the pair had just got back from fitting a false ceiling in a Saudi Arabian dental clinic and the row kicked off over Razzle seeing a supposed salt-beef bar in Jeddah (about as likely as seeing Trigger on *Mastermind*). Harris also was in partnership with Trigger, which is referred to by DI Slater in 'May the Force be with You'; he also flogs Del some log-effect gas fires in 'Strangers on the Shore'.

Iggy Higgins: A London bank robber, from whom Del borrows the sawn-off shotgun which he uses at the Duke of Maylebury's shooting party in 'A Royal Flush'.

Captain Kenworthy: Albert's old sea captain, who wore the wig which saved Albert's life. Stranded on an island in the Pacific during the Second World War, the natives were getting very restless. In an attempt to calm them, Kenworthy whipped off his wig, only to be shot by the islanders who "thought the wig had magical powers" and ran away to hold a ceremony, allowing Albert and the rest of the crew to "have it away on their toes". Kenworthy also crops up in 'Time On Our Hands' as Albert mentions him while chatting to Del about creating a counter worry for Rodney. The character was named after Christopher Kenworthy, one of the first showbiz journalists to write positively about the show.

Albie Littlewood: Del Boy's best friend in his youth. He died in 1965 when his bicycle fell on the live rail. Del believed he was taking a shortcut to meet up with him, but he was actually on his way to see Del's bird (behind his back) June Snell!

Ugandan Morris: A business contact of Del Boy's, he thinks Ugandan Morris is an exporter, but Rodney tells him he is actually an ex-porter! In the same scene, Del also learns that he's been deported, along with all of Del's gold identity bracelets!

Ronnie Nelson: The owner of Ron's Cash & Carry, although Del convinces him to rename it The Advanced Electronics Research and Development Centre, while selling him a Queen's Award for Industry plaque. Ronnie has the last laugh though, as he flogs Del 50 video recorders for £50 each, but they only work on the continent. Over the years he also sells Del 650 Russian army camcorders and a dodgy answerphone.

Sunglasses Ron: He is also involved with Paddy the Greek in the deal for the lead from the church roof, while his name also appears in 'To Hull and Back' on a list of those suspected of involvement in the diamond smuggling racket.

PUBLIC HOUSE

For series six, which saw the show in a new 50-minute format, the BBC switched the show to a Sunday night and John Sullivan later revealed he got letters from pub landlords asking him not to make the show so funny, because people were staying at home to watch the show and they were losing trade – by the end of that series, many pubs up and down the country were advertising screenings of the episodes, in much the same way pubs do with sports events.

TROTTER'S VARIOUS VEHICLES

Over the years the Trotters had an array of different vehicles, during the first series they're seen driving a Vauxhall Velox – only ever seen (and sold) in the episode 'Cash and Curry' – and the yellow three-wheeled van – which is often mistaken for a Reliant Robin, but is actually a Reliant Regal Supervan III. Series one also sees Del purchase a Ford Cortina (mark II) for £25 from Boycie and sell it on for £199! Later Del also purchases a Capri Ghia from the second-hand car salesman, which was due for scrapping before Boycie flogs it to Del Boy, who thinks it "handles like Maradona" (in reference to Argentinian footballer Diego Maradona's handball-goal against England in the 1986 World Cup Finals). The car is quickly christened the prat mobile by Rodders. Boycie also supplies Del's Rolls Royce, purchased after the boys make their millions in 'Time On Our Hands'. However it is the trademark yellow van which is by and far and away the most-recognisable vehicle, not only in the show, but also in the history of British television. In one episode Rodney jokes that he's looked everywhere to find spares for it, including archaeologists, but ironically that isn't too far from the truth! Over the twenty-plus years of *Only Fools & Horses* a meticulous amount of planning and preparation went into one of the most important props in the show, as the BBC got though a fair few different three-wheeled vans – as it was often more economical to source a new one than get the old ones through an MOT. They were usually rented from London firm Action Cars, and properties buyer in the early days of *Only Fools & Horses,* Chris Ferriday, revealed: "The chassis used to give out and they weren't worth repairing." As vehicles were changed, various items were retained for continuity purposes – seats, steering wheels and even the sign-written side panels and back door. Similarly with the Capri Ghia, three were required over the years, after the first began to disintegrate between series; again some of the signature items were transferred to the new vehicle and after the Trotters became millionaires, the third and final Capri was sold to fan Ian Nixon, who loaned it back to the BBC for the new millennium three-parter.

Three-wheeled van	*APL 911H/DHV 938D*
Ford Cortina	*OXL 825E*
Vauxhall Velox	*DJH 921B*
Ford Capri Ghia	*UYD 177R/CCR 412W*
Del's Rolls Royce	*1 DEL*
Rodney's Jaguar XK8	*A3 TWR*

* A limo version of the three-wheeled van was also used in a trailer for 'If They Could See Us Now…!', but this was camera trickery created by special effects firm Condor Post Production, who used a shot of the van in Monte Carlo to create a three-wheeler limo!

WALL STREET INFLUENCE

Just as the charcter of Del is influenced by the movie *Wall Street* in series six, John Sullivan's writing was also influenced by the film, starring Michael Douglas as the hard-nosed stock market trader Gordon Gekko. Sullivan saw the movie, just before penning the sixth series, and then set about decking out Derek in a striped shirt, red braces and trendy raincoat, topped off with aluminium brief case and filofax. He didn't have enough bunce to afford a Mercedes, but that didn't stop him giving people the impression he drove one, by carrying the company's key ring. Sullivan explained, "Del always thought he was a trend setter and of course he'd always get the trends wrong. Yuppies were big at the time so Del moved into that image. I also saw the film *Wall Street* and knew that if Del had seen it then it would have had a big impact on his life and he'd be straight out the following day to buy a pair of red braces and a smart shirt. So we got rid of the camelhair coat and smartened up his image, giving him a green mac, an aluminium briefcase and a mobile phone - but we kept the yellow van."

BIOGRAPHY: NICK LYNDHURST

Born on 20th April 1961 in Emsworth close to the Hampshire-Sussex border, Nicholas Lyndhurst grew up in East Wittering in West Sussex. Lyndhurst caught the acting bug at an early age: he was eight years old when he asked his mother Liz Long (a dancer at his father's holiday camp) if he could go to acting school and his mother enrolled him as a child student at Corona Stage Academy in West London. The academy was run by Rona Knight – but closed in 1989. After graduating through the academy he appeared in several television commercials and BBC Schools productions in the early-1970s. A few quieter years followed as he took his O levels before he landed his first major mainstream role. It was playing 17-year-old Adam in the popular BBC sitcom *Butterflies,* written by Carla Lane, that he first came to national prominence – and it was this character which sprung into Ray Butt's mind when casting Lyndhurst in the role of Rodney Trotter. Before that, he went on to play the teenage son of *Porridge's* 'Fletch', played by Ronnie Barker, in the short-lived spin-off series *Going Straight,* before achieving stardom in the series *Only Fools & Horses.* During his time on *Only Fools & Horses,* Lyndhurst also appeared in ITV's *The Two of Us, The Piglet Files,* and played the lead character of Gary Sparrow in the BBC's time-travel World War Two sitcom *Goodnight Sweetheart.* Between 1997 and 1999, Nicholas Lyndhurst was the public face of WHSmith, starring in the stationers' TV adverts as all four members of one family - and won a BAFTA for his acting in the ads. He is great friends with David Jason off screen, as he explained in the book *The Only Fools & Horses Story,* "We hit it off from day one and I think that was down to luck and chemistry. I had been told that David might be difficult to work with. I work with him fine so maybe I am a bit difficult to work with as well. *Only Fools* has always been a very happy show to work on. I was 19 when I started on it and 35 when I finished and that covered some very formative years and I do miss it. I will always miss it." Away from the screen and the stage, and similarly to his co-star Jason, Lyndhurst shuns the showbiz limelight and enjoys his privacy at his family home in West Sussex, where he lives with wife Lucy – a former ballet dancer – and their young son. His career record is listed on the page opposite.

Television

Heidi 1974
Anne of Avonlea..1975
Peter Pan 1976
The Prince and the Pauper....................................1976
Our Show..1977
Butterflies 1978-1983
Play of the Week: Fairies 1978
Going Straight 1978
Spearhead...1978
The Tomorrow People 1978
Father's Day...1979
To Serve Them All My Days.....................................1980
Only Fools and Horses.................................... 1981-2003
Play for Today: A Mother Like Him..........................1982
It'll All Be Over in Half an Hour............................1983
The Kenny Everett Christmas Show 1984
The Lenny Henry Show................................. 1984-1985
Round and Round..1984
Slimming Down..1984
The Two of Us 1986
The Piglet Files...1990
Goodnight Sweetheart 1993-1999
Stalag Luft...1993
Gulliver's Travels 1996
David Copperfield...1999
Thin Ice 2000
Murder in Mind..2003
The Children's Party at the Palace 2006
After You've Gone 2007-

Films

Endless Night...1971
Bequest to the Nation..1973
Bullshot 1983
Sky Bandits...1986
Lassie...2005

TROTTERS' INDEPENDENT TRADERS
VARIOUS STOCK LIST

ITEM   SOURCE IF KNOWN

ARMY-GRADE CAMCORDERS.........RUSSIA
BARKING DOGS..........................
BETATIME RADIO ALARM CLOCKS...LATVIA
BLOW-UP ADULT DOLLS...........LONDON
CHARLES & DI WEDDING PLATES.........
CHRISTMAS TREES X 30................
CRICKET BATS (SIGNED).............
CROWNING GLORY WIGS...........LONDON
CUTLERY SETS.........................
DEEP-SEA DIVERS' WATCHES............
DISPOSABLE LIGHTERS.................
EXCLUSIVE WOMEN'S FASHIONS.........
EXPORT-ONLY GIN....................UK
FACIAL SAUNAS X 2..................
FORD CORTINA MK II............BOYCIE
FUTAFAX MACHINES...................
GEORGIAN DIGITAL CLOCKS............
GENUINE MINK COATS.........ETHIOPIA
GLEN MCDONALD WHISKY........MALAYSIA
GROSS OF ITALIAN SHIRTS.....MALAYSIA
HAIRDRYERS..........................
HOME SOLARIUM......................
HOOKIE WATCHES..............TRIGGER

```
ID BRACELETS.........................
LUMINOUS YELLOW PAINT.................
INFRAMAX DP MASSAGER..................
KIDDIES' DOLLS..........GREAT BRITAIN
LADIES' ELECTRIC RAZORS...............
LOUVRE DOORS X 165....................
MOON-ROOF FOR A PEUGEOT...............
MUSICAL CHINA CATS....................
MUSICAL DOORBELLS.....................
MUSTAPHA CAR RADIOS...........ALBANIA
NOMAD CORDLESS PHONES.................
ORANGES.......................SEVILLE
PERFUME........................LONDON
POSEIDON ADVENTURE ON BETAMAX.......
RAJAH COMPUTERS......................
RED HORSE-RIDING HELMETS.............
RUBIK CUBES X 2 GROSS................
TELESCOPIC CHRISTMAS TREES...........
TIGHTS........................FRANCE
TOMATOES.......................JERSEY
SKI EQUIPMENT....................FIJI
SPACE INVADERS GAME..................
SUNTAN LOTION
VAN-LOAD OF ONE-LEGGED TURKEYS....UK
VIDEO RECORDERS.......................
VINYL BRIEFCASES X 25.......FAR EAST
WATER-DAMAGED SLEEPING BAGS X 5.....
WINE (RIESLING).............ROMANIAN
```

BRASS MONKEYS

In 'The Jolly Boys' Outing' when Del turns up at Raquel's flat in the early hours of the morning, he tells her that he's so cold he's just bumped into a brass monkey crying his eyes out. A random phrase it may seem, but it's actually born out of the old saying: 'It's cold enough to freeze the balls off a brass monkey'. This is a nautical saying which derives from a time when brass holders were used so sailors could safely stack pyramids of cannonballs on sailing ships. Brass was used to make the plates, because the balls would have rusted onto an iron plate in sea conditions, but problems still arose in very cold conditions – which would cause the brass plate to contract and the balls to roll off… hence the saying.

SIR DRISCOLL

Before they actually appeared in the final episode of the sixth series, the fearsome gangster brothers the Driscolls were mentioned in dispatches - most notably in the Christmas Special 'The Frog's Legacy', when Del tells Rodney and Albert he went to see them for information on the lost gold bullion they're searching for; when Albert asks what they're like, Rodney refers to them as being like the two Ronnies… "Biggs and Kray!" So viewers have an idea of the brothers before they actually appear in the show during 'Little Problems', when they come looking for Del, chasing the two grand he owes to them for 50 mobile phones; which unbeknown to Derek had arrived in Titco's possession from the Driscolls – via Mickey Pearce and his business partner Jevon. The part of elder brother Danny was actually specially created by writer John Sullivan for Sir Anthony Hopkins, after the esteemed actor revealed to Terry Wogan on his BBC chat show that he was a huge fan of the show, and would love to appear in it. Sadly when it came to filming Hopkins was double-booked. "He was in America," explained Sullivan, "filming some movie called *The Silence of the Lambs*!" Hopkins – who later penned the foreword for the BBC book *The Only Fools & Horses Story* – won the Best Actor Oscar for his role as Hannibal Lector, while Roy Marsden proved an exceptional replacement for the Hollywood star, and stepped in to make the role of Danny Driscoll his own.

SIMILES AND METAPHORS

John Sullivan wrote some fantastic metaphors and similes over the years, often used as insults... here are some of the best ones:

"That's like trusting a piranha fish with yer finger."
Del talking about Grandad working as a security guard.

"My belly's going up and down like Tower Bridge."
Rodney feels sick after a night out drinking.

"The night was blacker than a bailiff's heart."
Albert describes what was obviously a very dark night.

"You're as much use as a pair of sunglasses on a bloke with one ear."
Del on Grandad.

"That's like asking McDonalds to look after your cow."
Del on Albert's offer to look after Raquel and Damien while he goes away.

"You couldn't sell a black car to a witch."
Del on Rodney's sales technique and gift of the gab.

"There's more life in one of his meat pies."
Del Boy on a very quiet Nag's Head

"They were about as exciting as a Buddhist's hen night."
Del on Rodney's Christmas parties

"You've got a mind like a brown paper envelope."
Del on Rodney's mucky thoughts.

"You look like a mugger's pension scheme."
Rodney on Del's jewellery.

"It's like being mugged by a magistrate."
Del after Grandad accepts a tenner as a Christmas present and then lectures him on the commercialisation of Christmas

ONLY FOOLS TO EASTENDERS

Several *Only Fools & Horses* actors have ended up on Albert Square, inthe soap opera *Eastenders*. The most notable characters from the long-running BBC soap to have first appeared in *Only Fools & Horses* are Clyde Tavernier, Charlie Slater, Max Branning, Jim Branning, Rosie Miller and Tariq Larousi. Steven Woodcock played Jevon, Mickey Pearce's pal and business partner, in three episodes in the sixth series, and appeared in Christmas specials 'Dates' and 'The Jolly Boys' Outing'. In 1993 he landed the role of Clyde Tavernier in *Eastenders*, the barman in the Queen Vic falsely accused of murdering Eddie Royale. Gerry Cooper (Rosie) appeared as Lisa, Trigger's niece, who arranges for Del to have a go in a hang-glider in 'Tea for Three' and gets married to Andy in the 'Frog's Legacy'. Jake Wood (Max) played Rodney's gormless trainee in the computer section of Alan Parry's printing firm in 'The Jolly Boys' Outing'. John Bardon (Jim) was the security guard in 'The Longest Night'. Derek Martin (Charlie) played Arthur, one of the neighbours awoken by Del singing 'One Voice Singing in the Darkness' in the episode 'Fatal Extraction'. Nabil Elouahabi (Tariq) played Gary, the Frenchman accidentally kidnapped by Del, Rodney, Denzil and Trigger at a wine and beer warehouse in the episode 'Strangers on the Shore'.

700 MEGAWATT CUPPA

At the end of the first part of the two-part 1991 Christmas special 'Miami Twice', shown on Christmas Eve, a number of the 17.7 million viewers switching on their kettles for a brew caused a huge 700 megawatt power surge on the national grid!

CUSHTY

A favourite expression of Del's is cushty (also spelt kushti or kushty) which is a word strongly used by the Romany community and working classes prior to its popularisation by its frequent occurrences during *Only Fools & Horses*. It was a term which has its origins within the British Army. When soldiers were given the relatively easy posting to a British Army base at Cushtabar, it became known as a 'cushty'.

POLICEMEN & WOMEN

Policemen are Del's nemesis and a number of coppers - some friendly, some otherwise – appeared in the show over the years: Rodney dated one, Grandad got nicked by a Spanish one (not listed below as we actually don't see him being lifted), and Del even outwitted one over a stolen microwave!

PC Eric .... The Russians are Coming
WPC Sandra .... The Long Legs of the Law
River Policeman... Ashes to Ashes
DI Roy Slater* ....May the Force Be With You
PC Terry Hoskins* ....May the Force Be With You
PC who warns of the escaped convict .... Friday the 14th
Sergeant who tells Rod he's got the wrong man ..... Friday the 14th
PC who chases Del.. Healthy Competition
PC called by Rodney ....It's Only Rock and Roll
PC Parker .... To Hull and Back
PC scares off the brass at the station .... Dates
WPC whose shirt is ripped open by Del .... Dates
PC with WPC listed above .... Dates
Sergeant arrests Rodney in ....The Jolly Boys' Outing
PC with sergeant listed above......................The Jolly Boys' Outing
Mounted policeman .... Fatal Extraction
Number of PCs on riot patrol .... Fatal Extraction

*Slater and Hoskins – by then both promoted, Slater to Chief Inspector
– also appear in the Christmas Special 'To Hull and Back'.*

DEL BOY'S DAD

Peter Woodthorpe is superb as Del's dad in the episode 'Thicker Than Water' – but it wasn't just his acting skills which landed him the role. A likeness to David Jason was also a key factor in the casting. At this point viewers are also led to believe he's Rodney's dad too – but in the episode 'Sleepless in Peckham' learn otherwise. The casting decision also suggests John Sullivan was already thinking ahead to the final episode.

DEL BOY'S DRINKS

Del Boy's love of flamboyant cocktails is one of his recurring distinguishing trademarks. The Pina Colada is his favourite, usually covered in decorative fruits, umbrella and complete with translucent straws, and he is partial to a Tia Maria and Lucozade or a Singapore Sling – but as the episodes go on, he gets much more adventurous. Here are a few of his favourite exotic tipples:

Caribbean Stallion...Go West Young Man
Shots of tequila, coconut rum and crème de menthe; a smidgen of Campari; the merest suggestion of angostura bitters; topped up with fresh grapefruit juice; shaken, not stirred and poured slowly over broken ice.

Blackcurrant and Pernod........................The Second Time Around
When he bumps into his ex Pauline in the Nag's Head, Del's just ordered. He takes a gulp, for Dutch courage, before an embrace with his old-flame; most of the drink ends up on their lips! Shot of Pernod and shot of blackcurrant.

Pina Colada (but gets a Mackeson)........A Slow Bus to Chingford
Perhaps Del's favourite cocktail, but when he sends Grandad to the pub for the drinks he ends up with a can of Mackeson's Stout instead! A shot of tequila, a shot of coconut rum and a shot of crème de menthe

Remi Martin with cream soda and lots of ice........Christmas Crackers
Del and Rodney are out for a drink on Christmas Day at the Monte Carlo Club in New Cross when he orders this one. A shot of Remy Martin, poured over broken ice and topped up with cream soda.

Baileys and Cherryade..Heroes and Villains
The thought is enough to turn anyone's stomach, but Del with his cast-iron gullet, which can withstand even the dodgiest of mutton tikkas, doesn't care. One shot of Baileys, topped up with a splash of cherryade.

Harvey Wallbanger..Modern Men
Del has one of these to celebrate the news that Cassandra is expecting. Mix three shots of vodka with six of orange juice, then float a shot of Vanilla Galliano on top. Garnish with a slice of orange and a cherry.

Banana Daiquiri ....Who Wants to be a Millionaire
A shot-and-a-half of light rum, a dash of triple sec, one banana, a shot-and-a-dash of lime juice, one teaspoon of sugar. Blended together and topped off with a cherry!

Malibu Reef...Little Problems
Del is drinking this when the Driscolls come looking for him at the Nag's Head. A secret-recipe Trotter original!

Peach Daiquiri .... The Sky's the Limit
A shot-and-a-half of light rum, a shot of peach schnapps, a dash of apricot brandy, a cup of tinned peaches, a shot-and-a-dash of lime juice, one teaspoon of sugar. Blended together and topped off with a cherry!

Beaujolais Nouveau ....Yuppy Love
Del's trying to impress a couple of yuppy sorts in a trendy wine bar – but lets himself down when he tells the barman he wants a "seventy-nine".

Singapore Sling .... Dates
Eight parts gin, four parts cherry brandy, a shot of Cointreau, a shot of DOM Bénédictine, two shots of grenadine, sixteen parts pineapple juice, six parts lemon juice, a dash of Angostura bitters. Shaken. Great with a ham sarnie!

LICENSED TO DRILL

'Licensed To Drill' was never aired on TV; it was an educational episode made for schools to give an insight into North Sea oil. The story is that Del is conned into buying an 'oil rig' which doesn't exist! The underlying tone is to educate, but the humour still shines through, including the superb one liner from Del, of Rodney: "An evening course in Binary Bingo and he thinks he's Magnus Mackeson." But perhaps the best moment is Del explaining how he bought the rig for £400: "He wanted $400 didn't he, but I told him no way my son! We deal in currency I understand." Grandad responds, "Bet that shook him." The episode, filmed in 1984 between the third and fourth series, was written by Brian Hague; although John Sullivan did sing the eponymous theme tune. It was also significant as Lennard Pearce's last-ever appearance as Grandad. A copy of the episode exists online at wikipedia.org.

AWARDS

Only Fools & Horses is widely regarded as the nation's favourite comedy by the general public, but equally the critics love it too. The show has clocked up a number of awards over the years, including:

TRIC Television Situation Comedy of the Year............ 1984, 1987
BAFTA Best Comedy Series 1986, 1988, 1997
SOS Award for Funniest TV Programme 1989
Royal Television Society's Best Comedy Drama 1997
Writers' Guild of Great Britain Award (John Sullivan) 1997
NTA Most Popular Comedy Performer (David Jason)...... 1997, 2002

CHANGING TABLES

One thing viewers will have noticed over the years is that the gear in the Trotters' living room tends to change from episode to episode. The room is piled high with a range of hookie gear, damaged stock and just plain old junk, from damaged telephones to fridges full of tomatoes: this was done to reflect the fact that everything was available at a price! Perhaps one of the best examples of this was the fact that the living room table and chairs were changed for each episode: teak, oak, wicker, pine, formica, they all appeared – and of course when Raquel's folks come to stay in the episode 'Time On Our Hands', Del has to get hold of a decent dining table and famously borrows the massive one from the town hall, which only just fits into the Trotters' living room.

ALRIGHT DAVE

It's obvious from the first series that Roadsweeper Trigger isn't the sharpest tool in the box, but his continual misunderstanding over Rodney's name is a constant reminder to viewers of his rank stupidity. It's the classic running gag in the show's history, but it reached new levels when Nag's Head landlord Mike asks Trig what Del and Raquel are going to name the baby. "If it's a girl they're calling her Sigourny after an actress; and if it's a boy they're naming it Rodney... after Dave," explains Trigger!

FRENCH PHRASES I

Rodney tells Del Boy his French phrases might impress those down the market or the Nag's Head – but they have also left a lasting impression on the British public. Writer John Sullivan based the idea on an old associate, who would use Latin sayings in a similar manner, in order to impress. Listed below are Del's favourite phrases from the first series:

Big Brother

Phrase	*Del's translation/correct translation*
S'il vous plait	Look at me/If you please
Bonjour Trieste	You must be joking/Hello Trieste
Mal de mer	Impressive/Seasickness

Go West Young Man

Mon dieu	Goodness gracious/Goodness gracious
Son et luminaire	Beautiful/His and lamp
C'est la vie	That is life/That is life
Garcon la petite pois	Waiter, can I order?/Waiter, the peas

Cash and Curry

Pas de Basque	Whatever/No tail
Bouilla baise mon ami	What will be, will be/Fish stew my friend

Second Time Around

Pas de Calais	Delicious/Not Calais
Champs Élysées	Lovely, nice/French landmark
Manière d'être	Fire away/Handle for being

A Slow Bus to Chingford

Allemagne, dix points	Of course/Germany, ten points
Au contraire	On the contrary/ On the contrary

Christmas Crackers

Sacré-bleu [chef]	a top [chef]/gosh, blimey
Bain marie	Fantastic/Double boiler
Vin ordinaire	A top wine/table wine

RADIO TROTTER

Four episodes of *Only Fools & Horses* were re-edited for radio and broadcast on BBC Radio 4 in June and July 1999. The episodes were 'The Long Legs of the Law', 'A Losing Streak', 'No Greater Love' and 'The Yellow Peril'. These episodes and three other audio box-sets have since been released on CD.

TROTTER TAKEAWAYS

The Trotters – particularly Del – are more than partial to a takeaway dinner; here are a few of the family's favourite Chinese and Indian establishments:

The China Gardens Takeaway
The Golden Dragon
The Golden Lotus
The Light of Nepal
The Star of Bengal

HE WHO DARES

"He who dares, wins" is one of Del Boy's choice phrases, which he often utters as he dives head first into a business deal. It derives from the motto: 'Who Dares Wins', originally used by the British Special Air Service; nine special armed forces élite units across the world have since adopted it:

Country	Unit
United Kingdom	Special Air Service
Greece	Hellenic Special Forces
Australia	Special Air Service Regiment
New Zealand	Special Air Service
France	First Marine Infantry Parachute Regiment
Cyprus	Tactical Group
Israel	Sayeret Matkal
Sri Lanka	Sri Lanka Army Commando Regiment
Belgium	Belgian First Parachute Battalion

BIOGRAPHY: LENNARD PEARCE

Born on 9th February 1915, Lennard Pearce studied at the Royal Academy of Dramatic Art. In the 1930s he toured Germany, where he met Hitler at a theatre in Berlin and later told Nicholas Lyndhurst: "Knowing what I do now, what I wouldn't have given for a gun." He served with the army's entertainment unit during the Second World War and most of his professional life was spent on the stage. He made his TV debut in the 1960s as an ambulanceman in an epsiode of *No Hiding Place* and also had bit parts in *Dixon of Dock Green* and the famous Wednesday Play *Cathy Come Home* – and after landing the role of Grandad, also appeared in an episode of ITV's *Minder* – but like so many in the show, it was for his role in *Only Fools & Horses* that he is best remembered by the British public. "I have never been in a hit series before and it's nice being recognised," he once told the *News of the World*. He also told the newspaper he had doubts about the quality of the third series, "The first two were so well constructed I didn't think John Sullivan could keep it up but I was wrong. The standards are just as high and I aim to be around if there is a fourth series." Sadly, Lennard died shortly after filming had begun on the fourth series. He suffered a major heart attack and died in hospital a few days later on 14th December 1984. He had already filmed some scenes for the episode 'Hole in One'; his character was replaced by Buster Merryfield, who came into the show as Grandad's long-lost brother.

TITLE SEQUENCE

The opening credits of *Only Fools & Horses* feature images of the three main actors peeling on and off the screen sequentially like sticky labels, appearing over photographs of everyday life in 1980s London, including the tower block in Acton, which was first used as Nelson Mandela House. The sequence was conceived by Peter Clayton as a "metaphor for the vagaries of the Trotters' lifestyle". Through the years, the title sequence was updated with new footage, but it only ever featured Del, Rodney and either Grandad or Uncle Albert. The shots of Del and Rodney were updated three times during the series' run to reflect their ageing, whilst Grandad and Uncle Albert only ever received one version each.

CHARLADY

In the episode 'Yesterday Never Comes' (the one in which Del hooks up with the 'posh tart' antiques dealer Miranda to restore his 'Queen Anne' cabinet) we learn that Del's gran was a charlady. Younger viewers of the show may never have heard of such a thing – but a charlady was a house cleaner, and the word was well-known in the mid-twentieth century. Unlike a maid or housekeeper, which were typically live-in positions, the charlady worked for weekly wages and usually came and went on a daily basis. Del's gran was a charlady to an art dealer, from whom she nicked the painting which Miranda tricks Del into giving her for her birthday.

YOU'RE NICKED

A number of actors and extras who appeared in *Only Fools & Horses* went on to work on other shows, but two ended up in ITV's hit *The Bill*. Graham Cole is seen inspecting the Trotters' passports in the episode 'It Never Rains...'. While Nula Conwell played Nag's Head barmaid Maureen. Cole went on to play the long-running part of friendly PC Tony Stamp, while Conwell played WDC Viv Martello; her character was shot dead in the series during 1993.

COMEDY PLAYHOUSE

John Sullivan first got the bug for writing scripts after seeing the pilot episode of *Steptoe & Son* 'The Offer' on BBC's *Comedy Playhouse*. Sullivan was taken by the humour and pathos of the show and that was where he got the urge to write.

STANDING OVATION

The final episode of the 1996 trilogy saw the brothers finally become millionaires, as they auction off the Lesser watch for £6.2m. In the episode the boys receive a standing ovation when they next visit the Nag's Head – and on an emotional evening at BBC Television Centre the cast also received a standing ovation from the studio audience after filming the final scene.

THE CHANDELIER SCENE

It is widely regarded by fans as one of the most-famous, funniest and all-time favourite moments in the show's history – but setting up the famous chandelier scene in the episode 'A Touch of Glass' proved a tough task for *Only Fools & Horses* producer Ray Butt. First of all he and his production team had to find a location; and it wasn't easy to find a venue where owners would let them drop a heavy cut-glass chandelier from a great height onto the floor below! Clayesmore School near Blandford Forum eventually proved the perfect setting. Then the props department had to pay for a replica chandelier, which took a large portion of the budget of the whole series and actually cost more than the original! Meaning the final scene had to be shot in one take, and left David Jason and Nicholas Lyndhurst under enormous pressure not to laugh until the cut. Ray Butt even threatened Lyndhurst with the sack if he laughed, telling him: "If you laugh when it's dropped we've lost the end scene; if we've lost the end scene we've lost the episode; if we've lost the episode we've lost the series, because the BBC will only transmit six. So if you laugh when that drops I will fire you!" Thankfully there was no need for that as the take was perfect, with Jason and Lyndhurst sailing through with ease to create a hilarious moment of television history.

RODNEY'S HUMILIATIONS

A series or Christmas special would rarely pass without Rodney either humiliating himself or being humiliated by his older brother Del. From chief mourner to being burnt to a shade of red on the home solarium, Nicholas Lyndhurst was perfect playing the straight man Rodney in these situations:

Works as a night watchman.....................A Slow Bus to Chingford
Gets sunburned .... Tea for Three
Dresses like a wally..A Royal Flush
Works as a chief mourner .... The Frog's Legacy
Joins the Groovy Gang...........................The Unlucky Winner is...
Models horrible ski wear .... Fatal Extraction
Dresses up as a Roman gladiator ...... If They Could See Us Now...!

RODNEY'S REVENGE

Rodney only really gets his revenge on Del Boy in one episode 'Tea for Three' – and almost instantly regrets it. The boys are both smitten by Trigger's niece Lisa, and after Del leaves him to burn under the home solarium, Rodney gets his revenge by arranging for his older brother to go hang gliding. Del's macho pride gets the better of him and he's left with no choice but to go flying. He eventually crash lands and Del attempts to have the last laugh at Rodney's expense by making him think he's been left paralysed.

ALBERT'S REASSURANCE

While Del and Rodney are away in Miami, Raquel and Cassandra are at home worrying about the brothers. The brothers can't phone home because they're told the phone lines were down due to a tropical storm, and believe they can't contact anyone in England. Cassandra is away in Eastbourne, on work duty with the bank, when she telephones the flat for news. Uncle Albert in a poor attempt to reassure her everything is alright tells her that the campervan, which Del and Rodney had hired in the States, has been found… broken into and abandoned!

ONLY FOOLS TOP 40

In the run up to Christmas 2006, UK Gold held an internet poll to discover viewers' top 40 *Only Fools & Horses* moments. The full list is below, but three of the most famous scenes in the show finish in the top three positions. First is the moment when Del Boy falls through the open bar while drinking with Trigger in a wine bar – expertly shot in one take. Second was the chandelier scene, in which Grandad is working on a different chandelier to the boys, who are waiting to catch the another one as the other comes crashing to the floor! Third was the hilarious scene that saw Del and Rodney foil a mugging, running through the backstreets of Peckham, dressed as Batman & Robin.

40	Del's Shooter
39	Canary

LOCATIONS

All of the indoor scenes were filmed at the BBC studios, but most of the outdoor 'on-location' shoots were filmed nearby to BBC headquarters in West London, until the show moved to Bristol because of its popularity in London. Below is a list of some of the locations used throughout the seven series and beyond.

Big Brother

Market scenes...Chapel Market, Islington
The Nag's Head..The Alma Pub, Islington

Cash and Curry

Chamber of Trade Dinner...................Cuckoo Hill Community Centre

A Slow Bus to Chingford

Tyler Street Garage..............Grey-Green Coach Station, Stamford Hill

Ashes to Ashes

Peckham Bowling Club ....Hanwell Bowling Green

The Yellow Peril

Cemetery where mother is buried ....Walpole Park, Ealing
The Golden Lotus ....A café in Hanwell

It Never Rains...

Spanish Hotel ....Knoll House Hotel, Dorset

A Touch of Glass

Hall at which auction is held.............Sutton Waldron Village Hall
Ridgemere Hall .... Claymore School, Iwerne Minster

Homesick

Community Hall ....St Nicholas' Church Hall, Chiswick

Friday the 14th

Boycie's Cottage .... A cottage in Iwerne Minster
Police Station...A house in Iwerne Minster

Strained Relations

Grandad's funeral ....Field Road Cemetery, Hammersmith

Hole in One

Pub cellar.. Kensal Road
Magistrates' Court ....Kingston Magistrates' Court

Sleeping Dogs Lie

Boycie's front garden and other scenes ....Harrow-on-the-Hill

As One Door Closes

The park where the butterfly is caught... Ravenscroft Park, London

To Hull and Back

Train station ....Hull Station
Amro Bank, Amsterdam.................................. Barclays Bank, Hull

The Miracle of Peckham

Church ....St Alphedge, King James St, Southwark

A Royal Flush

The Duke's estate....................................Clarendon Park, Wiltshire

The Frog's Legacy

Market scenes............................. Seymour Rd/Rectory Rd, Ipswich
Wedding reception .... Helmingham Hall
Church scenes.. St Mary's Church

Dates

Dating Agency ....Kelter Recruitment, Old Market Rd, Bristol
Car jump scene.. Talbot Road, Isleworth
Nag's Head exterior . The Waggon & Horses, Stapleton Rd, Bristol
Police station .... Winchmore Hill Police Station, London

Yuppy Love

Adult education centre exterior ......48 Queen Charlotte St, Bristol
Wine bar exterior .... The Old Granary, Welsh Back, Bristol
Nightclub ....Parkside Club, Bath Rd, Bristol

Danger UXD

Rodney dines with Cassandra..................... Parkside Hotel, Bristol
Nelson Mandela House............................Duckmore Road, Bristol
Dirty Barry's sex shop exterior.................... Hanover Street, Bristol
Explosion......................... British Gas Site, Canon's Marsh, Bristol

Chain Gang

The One Eleven Club....................Parkside Club, Bath Rd, Bristol
Restaurant .... Villa Verde, St Stephen's St, Bristol
Tandoori Nights ....King's Rd, Hammersmith

The Jolly Boys' Outing

Market scenes...............Dumpton Greyhound Stadium, Ramsgate
Station...Margate Station
The Halfway House..............................The Roman Galley, Chislet
Cassandra on the phone ....Marina Resort Hotel, Ramsgate
Coach explosion .... The Bungalow Car Park, Margate
Guest houses .... Dalby Square, Margate
Mardi Gras Club .... The Top Hat Club, Margate
Rodney's flat, exterior ....Rebecca Court, Margate

Rodney Come Home

Shopping centre... The Broadwalk, Bristol
Nightclub ....Parkside Club, Bath Rd, Bristol
Alan Parry's printing company .... Gemini, York St, Bristol

The Chance of a Lunchtime

Floating restaurant .... Shoots, Bristol
The Nag's Head, exterior ....The White Horse, Bedminster
Wine bar .... Henry's Africa Hothouse, Whiteladies Rd, Bristol

Stage Fright

Down by the Riverside ClubThe Courage Social Club, Bedminster
The Starlight Rooms ....The Locarno Club, Bristol

He Ain't Heavy, He's My Uncle

Scenes hunting for Albert...London
(including Tower Bridge, HMS Belfast and Portobello Rd)

Miami Twice

Christening scenes, interior ...... St John's Church, Ladbroke Grove
Christening scenes, exterior .... St John's Church, Kentish Town
Miami scenes .... on location in Miami

Mother Nature's Son

Myles' organic farm shop .... Swain's Farm Shop, Henfield
Allotment .... Natal Road, Lower Bevendean, Brighton
Hotel scene .... The Grand Hotel, Brighton

Fatal Extraction

Del and Rodney walk to the dentist ...... Brunswick Square, Bristol
Market scenes .... Ashton Gate, Bristol City FC
Casino .... The Old Granary, Welsh Back, Bristol

Heroes and Villains

Breakdown scene .... Bristol city centre shopping precinct
Council offices car park .... Bristol Coroner's Office, Upper York St
Batman and Robin run off .... York St, Bristol
Rodney chases the muggers .... Park Avenue, Bristol
Peckham Post Office .... St John's Lane Post Office, Bristol

Modern Men

Outside Nelson Mandela House .... Duckmore Road, Bristol
Hospital .... Ham Green Hospital

Time On Our Hands

Floating restaurant .... Shoots, Bristol
The Nag's Head, exterior .... The White Horse, Bedminster
Wine bar .... Henry's Africa Hothouse, Whiteladies Rd, Bristol

If They Could See Us Now...!

French hotel scene .... Hotel De Paris, Monte Carlo
Justin's office .... Council Chamber, Weston-Super-Mare
Two houses (funeral) .... Woodland Rd, Weston-Super-Mare
Restaurant (Rod & Cassandra) Dragon's Kiss, Weston-Super-Mare
Del and Rodney's taxi ride .... Shaftesbury Avenue, London
Goldrush .... Pinewood Studios, London

GRANDAD'S PASSING

Filming had begun for the fourth series a few weeks before Lennard Pearce suffered the heart attack which claimed his life. He was rushed to Whittington Hospital in Highgate, London – but on Sunday 16 December news reached Ray Butt that Lennard had died. Filming was scheduled to take place at 9am that day, but Butt greeted the cast and crew with the dreadful news, tears flowed, filming was cancelled and they were sent home. The decision was made that the series would continue, but neither Butt nor writer John Sullivan wanted a new actor to replace Grandad – despite pressure from BBC bosses. The pair held firm, as they felt Pearce had made the Grandad role his own. Therefore an uncle (or possibly aunt) would be brought in to replace Grandad. Eventually an aunt was ruled out, as it was felt that it would restrict the boys' mickey-taking and actions towards the elderly relative, and thus the character of Uncle Albert was born. Albert could replace Grandad in most episodes, but John Sullivan had the huge task of re-writing the scripts and writing two new episodes (it was felt the series couldn't start with a funeral), so 'Happy Returns' was written to only feature Del and Rodney (but had a mention of Grandad being in hospital), before Sullivan penned the brilliant 'Strained Relations' which featured Grandad's funeral. "The episode was superb," explained David Jason. "I don't think any other writer would have taken on the challenge that John did – to bury one of your central characters in a comedy series. It just doesn't happen. But he rose to that challenge and delivered in a brilliant script." So a few weeks after attending Lennard Pearce's funeral for real, several of the cast and crew were at his on-screen burial – which is believed to be a first in the history of British TV. Sullivan brilliantly turned the sombre mood as Rodney dropped what he believed to be Grandad's trilby into the grave, only for the vicar to ask, "Has anyone seen my hat?"

SIX DAMIEN DEREK TROTTERS

Six different actors have played Damien Trotter: five as he's grown up; and Douglas Hodge, who played grown-up Damien in Rodney's dream during 'Heroes and Villains'. They are: Patrick McManus (1991), Grant Stevens (1991), Robert Liddement (1992), Jamie Smith (1993–96), Douglas Hodge (1996, as adult), and Ben Smith (2001–03).

DEL'S GLOSSARY

Ajax: Dutch for hello, but also one of Amsterdam's football teams.

Ambiguous: Being able to use both hands to play volleyball and other things.

Bacon and the egg situation: The same as the chicken and the egg situation, but tastier in Del's book.

Di Stefano: Foreign for well done, bravo, excellent. Also a former Real Madrid player: Alfredo Di Stefano.

Gandhi's revenge: The inevitable dodgy stomach that follows after a ruby murray (curry).

It's epidemic: Set in stone, so there's little point discussing it.

Jarwohl: Yes in German.

King Farouk: The Anglo-Saxon who was best known for holding back the tide; not to be confused with King Canute – an Egyptian king. Rodney is always getting these two the wrong way round.

Kuvera: There are two Kuvera's in Del's life: one is a premier Indian wicketkeeper, the other is better known to most people as the God of Wealth in the second aspect of the Hindu Trimurti.

Monchengladbach: German for hello.

Non Compos Mentis: Drunk, and therefore not fully with it.

Puskas: Foreign for excellent! Possibly derives from Ferenc Puskas the excellent Hungarian footballer.

Stone me: English for mon dieu!

Tempus fugit: Latin for time flies.

TO HULL AND BACK - BUT ONLY JUST

Christmas wasn't Christmas for many years in the 1980s and 1990s without the feature-length *Only Fools & Horses*. It was more important to most than the Queen's Speech! But the first-ever Christmas special in 1985 nearly didn't happen for a number of reasons. Firstly the BBC had major concerns over the budget to make John Sullivan's script, which had the Trotters – Del, Rodney and Albert – smuggling diamonds back from Holland via a boat. Producer Ray Butt gave BBC bosses a projected budget and was told there was no way he would get the amount required. Butt's response: "If you can't afford that, then you ain't gonna get it." Filming scenes in Amsterdam which see the Trotter trio racing away from Dutch policemen (they mistakenly believe they're being chased when in fact the coppers are actually chasing another man) hiked up the cost and it looked as if the episode wouldn't be made. That was until Butt found himself at the same dinner table as the-then new BBC controller Michael Grade, at a TV festival in Switzerland. Seizing the moment, Butt told Grade of the predicament and the controller's intervention saved the show – and Butt didn't just get the £600,000 he needed for the episode, but an additional £250,000 on top! The episode was also notable for the fact that it was the first time the show hadn't been filmed in front of a live studio audience, and there was no time to add a laughter track; meanwhile the reason the Trotters' front room and Nag's Head look slightly different in this episode is that they were filmed in a special set built on location in Hull at Armstrong's (a former munitions factory) in the city.

CHAS & DAVE

When John Sullivan penned the theme tune for *Only Fools & Horses* he did it with Chas & Dave very much in mind. Sullivan was told the pair had been approached to sing it, but had refused, though Chas & Dave – huge fans of the show – when interviewed years later never recalled being asked. However, they did sing the closing theme 'Margate' for the classic Christmas episode 'The Jolly Boys' Outing' – and eventually got round to singing Sullivan's closing theme, doing a brilliant job, for the version which was used at the end of UKTV Gold's *Only Fools' Top 40 Moments* broadcast in December 2006.

BIT-PART APPEARED TWICE

John Pennington plays the vicar in both 'Christmas Trees', the short Christmas special shown in 1982, and in 'Strained Relations' the second episode of the fourth series. Meanwhile Dev Sagoo plays the Indian waiter in the curry house which features in the series two Christmas episode 'Diamonds are For Heather' and is back in the same role for 'Healthy Competition'.

ON THE FIRM

The following Peckham-based businesses popped up over the years in various episodes. Delaney's Club featured in the sketch during the Trotters' appearance at the Royal Variety Performance in 1986.

Boyce Auto Sales & Car Accessories
Delaney's Club
Eels On Wheels
Fatty Thumb Café
Patel's Multi-Mart
Peckham Car Rentals
Peckham Echo
Peckham Exhaust Centre
Ron's Cash & Carry
Transworld Express
Tyler Street Bus & Coach Garage

HOLE IN ONE

The episode in which Albert falls down the cellar (and Del attempts to sue the brewery for compensation) was originally written for Grandad. In the two weeks prior to Lennard Pearce's heart-attack and subsequent passing, he'd filmed several of the location scenes; most were re-shot with Buster Merryfield as Uncle Albert, but the scenes which saw Ken McDonald (Nag's Head landlord Mike) looking up from the cellar, were actually filmed with him looking at Lennard Pearce off camera. These were not reshot, but simply cut together with new scenes filmed with Buster Merryfield to make it look as if Mike is talking to Uncle Albert.

TROTTER COMPANIES

Del Boy is often coming up with schemes and plans which are going to make him and Rodney millionaires, and often these schemes involve him diversifying and setting up a new company or brand within the TITCO business empire. Over the years, viewers have seen the following Trotter companies and brands (NB: Trotter Air, Trotterex and Trotters' Meat Fingers only appear in one of Rodney's dreams):

Company/brand	Episode
Peckham Spring	Mother Nature's Son
Trotter Air	Heroes and Villains
Trotter Crash Turbans	Modern Men
Trotterex	Heroes and Villains
Trotter International Star Agency	Stage Fright
Trotter Oil	Licensed to Drill
Trotters' Ethnic Tours	A Slow Bus to Chingford
Trotters' Meat Fingers	Heroes and Villains
Trotters' Pre-Blessed Wine	Miami Twice
Trotter Watch	A Slow Bus to Chingford

OFF THE BOOKSHELF

There have been a number of books devoted to the trials and tribulations of the Trotter family and *Only Fools & Horses*. In addition several biographies have been written on David Jason; while Buster Merryfield wrote his autobiography *During The War - and Other Encounters*. The list below shows all of the specific *Only Fools & Horses* books:

The Trotter Way to Millions.. Guild Publishing/BBC Books, 1990
The Trotter Way to Romance ...... Weidenfeld and Nicholson,1991
The Location Guide .... Steve Clark, 1993
The Only Fools & Horses Story .... Steve Clark, 1998
The Bible of Peckham Volume I .... John Sullivan, 1999
The Bible of Peckham Volume II .... John Sullivan, 2000
The Bible of Peckham Volume III .... John Sullivan, 2001
The Complete A-Z of Only Fools & Horses... Richard Webber, 2002

A LUMPY ENGINE

There's a wonderful scene involving the Trotters' three-wheeled van in the feature-length 'Dates'. Del has just discovered Raquel is a part-time strip-o-gram (after hiring her as a birthday surprise for for Albert) and flees the Nag's Head. After rowing with Raquel in the pub car park he goes to start the van and the engine packs up (Rodney's been driving it at a fair old lick on his date with Nerys). Graham Brown was the visual effects expert who set up the scene. "I used a technique I developed whilst working on *Crackerjack* where I hung a bucket underneath the bonnet. The director wanted something visual as well as the sound of the engine playing up, so I bought some gravy browning, which was the only thing I could get hold of at the time, and put it into a bucket, together with some nuts and bolts. The bucket stood underneath the bonnet and connected to a piece of metal which came through into the cab, so when it was pulled, the bucket tipped and poured all the material out on to the floor!"

MENTIONED FIRST, SEEN SECOND

Like Sunglasses Ron and Paddy the Greek, both Marlene Boyce and Mickey Pearce started life as characters who were often heard of but never actually seen, as both were mentioned more than once before they actually appeared on screen. Marlene first crops up in conversation during 'Go West Young Man' as Boycie has to hide from her the E-type Jag he's bought his bit on the side; she also gets various mentions in 'A Losing Streak' and 'May The Force Be With You' – both referring to her reputation with the men. She finally appears in 'Sleeping Dogs Lie' during series four. Mickey Pearce also gets his first mention in the episode 'Go West Young Man': Rodney tells Del Boy that Mickey has been advising him over the trouble he's been having with his latest girlfriend Monica. It later transpires young Pearce has advised him on a trial separation so he can take Monica dancing. Mickey also lends Rodney a book on body language in 'Christmas Crackers' and his name crops up in 'No Greater Love'. Mickey finally appears during series three in 'Healthy Competition' as Rodney's partner in his newly-formed business venture, after splitting with Del and Trotters' Independent Traders.

ROYAL VARIETY PERFORMANCE

On 24th November 1986 – in between filming scenes for that year's Christmas special 'A Royal Flush' – Del, Rodney and Albert appeared in the Royal Variety Performance. The script was written that they had stumbled onto the stage at the Theatre Royal, Drury Lane after taking a wrong turn to deliver some booze to a pal of Del's called Chunky, who ran a West End nightclub. For one of the jokes Rodney looked up to the Royal Box and spotting it was occupied by the Queen Mother and the Duchess of York began to bow. Del Boy then asked Rodney, "What's the matter with you?" Looks to the box, and slightly dazzled by the lights asked, "Chunky, is that you?" As the sketch has unfolded this line had become a major source of concern to John Sullivan as he watched the show on TV at home. "When I wrote about Chunky I didn't know the Duchess of York was going to be there. It was before she'd joined Weightwatchers and in those days she had a few pounds on her. I was watching at home and thought 'Oh God' when I saw she was in the Royal Box!" The line brought the house down and thankfully the Royal Family (who are fans of the show) also saw the funny side: the Queen Mother even gave a Royal wave. After the show David Jason, Nicholas Lyndhurst and Buster Merryfield were presented to the Queen Mother, who stroked Buster's beard and commented, "So it is real then!"

POP GROUPS

Only Fools & Horses writer John Sullivan has come up with some rather inventive names for pop groups who appeared in the comedy show over the years. 'A Bunch of Wallies' are the group of which Rodney's a member in 'It's Only Rock and Roll'. They provide the music for St Patrick's Night at the Shamrock Club in Deptford, after the 'Dublin Bay Stormers' end up in prison. Meanwhile, in her younger days before she met Del, Raquel was once part of a singing duet (not the one she formed with singing roadsweeper Tony Angelino) called 'Double Cream'. She also sang at Talk of the Town in Reading, where she was top of the bill with Laurie London – although Del gets mixed up and thinks she was top of the bill with Otis Redding at Talk of the Town, London!

FOOLS RETURN?

In September 2007, Nicholas Lyndhurst admitted he would love to see *Only Fools & Horses* revived by the BBC. David Jason's co-star said he would love it if the sitcom returned. In an interview for the *Radio Times* he said, "I've always said I'd do another *Fools* tomorrow - but there are an awful lot of people involved in the decision-making. Lyndhurst also told the magazine that he doesn't mind people having a joke with him by calling him a plonker. "I have to say it's scaffolders and journalists that use it the most, but it's absolutely fine."

AFRICAN INFLUENCE

In 1980s Britain there was a tendency to name public buildings after famous Africans, and John Sullivan featured this when developing place names in *Only Fools & Horses* and that led to the following:

Desmond Tutu House
Jesse Jackson Memorial Hall
Martin Luther King Comprehensive
Nelson Mandela House
Zimbabwe House

PIZZA THE ACTION

It's funny how persuasive television advertising can be... John Sullivan wrote Mickey Pearce into the third series of *Only Fools & Horses* for the episode 'Healthy Competition'. Having read the script for the episode, producer Ray Butt had a mental picture in his mind of Pearce and couldn't believe his eyes when the vision came to life during a TV commercial for Pizza Hut! Butt spotted Patrick Murray playing a similar character to Mickey, trying to chat up a couple of girls and failing miserably, in the ad for the restaurant chain and immediately called him for an audition. "I saw Ray on the Friday... and I read a scene from 'Healthy Competition' and Ray said, 'Can you start Monday?' I was delighted and two days later found myself in Bournemouth filming my first episode." Up until then Murray was best known for his role in Alan Parker's film *Scum*.

RODNEY'S LOVE LIFE

Until Cassandra, Rodney's love life was a bit of a non-event. Del Boy once told him, "If they don't know Adam Ant's birthday or the Chelsea result, it's goodnight Vienna, innit?" He does pull a few birds now and then, but more often than not scares them off – either because he gets too heavy, or with his fetish for a woman in uniform!

Shanghai Lil: One of Rodney's early conquests, he met her at Basingstoke Art College, but the relationship ended when they were both caught smoking marijuana: Rodney was expelled and Lil deported.

Monica: She is described by Del as a 'little tart with fat thighs'. Things didn't work out and Mickey Pearce advised Rodney to take a two-week trial separation – she then started dating Mickey!

Janice: Rodney impresses by showing off his art, but Janice is a classy girl – who doesn't wear a bra! The relationship was going quite well, but fizzled out when Rodney began working as a Nocturnal Security Officer.

Sandra: The WPC who much to Del's chagrin Rodney takes to the pictures. The relationship is doomed the moment Rodney decides to bring her back to the flat, where she spots plenty of hookie gear!

Linda: After no success with Sandra, Rodney hooks up with Linda, but her parents put a stop to things after they arrive home early and find Rodney with his trousers on back to front!

Marguerite: The skinny bird from the dry cleaners, who Rodney dates just a few weeks before he became toy boy to Irene Mackay. He claims it wasn't love, but merely an infatuation.

Irene Mackay: An older woman, she was 40 when Rodney dated her, before Irene dumped him (at Del's request) and Rodney realised she was merely another infatuation... shame Del didn't too!

Zoe: The perfect way to get over his relationship with Irene! Rodney met Zoe at the Roller Disco. She was 18 years old and had a fabulous figure.

Bernice: Things were going okay with Bernice until she got too serious, forcing Rodney to put his foot down, because wherever he lays his hat, that's his home!

Debby: Pretty 18-year-old who worked in the local newsagents. Things went wrong for Rodney when Del thought she might be his niece. It turned out she wasn't, but by then she was dating Mickey Pearce!

Big Brenda: A disastrous blind date, set up by Del Boy, with the Southern Area Shot-put Champion. Rodney never saw her again, as he couldn't bear another evening of hearing her tales about Zola Budd.

Yvonne: Another set up by Del, unbeknown to Rodney. Despite telling everyone he and stripper Yvonne were thinking of getting engaged, it ended after one date... as she decided to do her stripping routine!

Imogen: Rodney thought she was getting serious, even talking about engagement, but just as he's wondering whether to end the relationship he spots Imogen out with another man... thus saving him the bother.

Helen: Rodney met her at the Nag's Head disco, and thought she looked like Linda Evans; Del didn't, calling her an old dog and nicknames her 'Helen of Croydon: the face that launched a thousand dredgers'.

Vicky: Posh bit of skirt, who was the daughter of the Duke of Malebury; She met Rodney in the market and the two began dating. All was going well until Del Boy began interfering in things.

Nervous Nerys: Quiet, shy and retiring type, but Jevon and Mickey tell Rodney she likes macho men. Their first date is a disaster with Rodney narrowly avoiding getting beaten up, hence things never advanced.

The ones that got away from Rodney include Lisa, Trigger's niece who both Del and Rodney made a play for, before discovering she was already engaged to Andy; and of course Tanya (or Miss Quick Fit, as Del calls her) the siren of the exhaust centre who Rodney, on the advice of Mickey Pearce, asked out in a very silly attempt to make Cassandra jealous!

LITTLE PROBLEMS

Possibly the most aptly named episode of all was 'Little Problems' - the final one of series six which saw Rodney finally tie the knot and marry Cassandra - because John Sullivan had to deal with one particular little problem before filming could commence. Five days before rehearsals began, Patrick Murray, who played Mickey Pearce, had a serious accident at home. He tripped over his dog and fell through a pane of glass, lacerating his arm so severely it could have cost him his life. He had five hours of neuro-surgery, lost five pints of blood and by all accounts was lucky not lose his hand. Thinking he'd either be written out of the script at worst, or at best, filming of his scenes would be put on hold, Patrick called the BBC to give them the bad news - but John Sullivan once again demonstrated his skill for scriptwriting by quickly rewriting the part of Mickey (and his oppo Jevon) to incorporate the plaster cast into the story line. "I couldn't believe it. I'd been feeling very down in hospital, not just from the pain, and the idea of going back to work really lifted me." Hence, when the pair turn up at the Nag's Head to warn Del he is facing a visit from London heavies the Driscoll brothers, Mickey's wearing a real plaster while Jevon's got a fake neck brace on and Del refers to their injuries and says it's a Driscoll trademark to leave the face alone, but "knock the 'ell out of the body".

DOUBLE EXPLOSION

One of the most memorable scenes in the history of the show is seeing the coach explode in 'The Jolly Boys' Outing', caused by Del's dodgy radio catching fire. The coach used for the episode was bought by the BBC in a Trotter-style deal for two grand, but had to pass an MOT and necessary safety tests in order to be used for the scenes en route to Margate. For the explosion, once in place, the BBC visual effects experts strapped tanks of petrol to the underside of the coach. The scene was filmed using three cameras at Bungalow Car Park in Margate's Palm Bay, with members of the Kent Fire Brigade on hand to extinguish the flames – and the coach was actually blown up more than once! Producer Gareth Gwenlan explained, "The fire brigade went in, put it out, and a while later we did it again."

BIOGRAPHY: BUSTER MERRYFIELD

Buster Merryfield, who played Uncle Albert, was born on 27th November 1920, and went from being a retired bank manager to becoming a national institution after joining *Only Fools & Horses* in 1984 – but looking back over his life it is no surprise that the previously unheard of actor (he'd only made a handful of television appearances before landing his part in the comedy) was such a success. His character of Uncle Albert effectively took over the role of senior citizen member of the Trotter family from the late Lennard Pearce, who had played Grandad. Albert was written into the show as Grandad's long-lost brother who returned to Peckham for his brother's funeral in the second episode of the fourth series 'Strained Relations'. Buster was born Harry Merryfield, in Battersea, South London; he attended Sir Walter St John's Grammar School. He was a keen sportsman throughout his life and became British schoolboy boxing champion in 1936 and later was Southern Command army champion in 1945. He also had a brief spell as a professional footballer with Millwall; he played one full first-team game for the club. Away from sport, he served with the Royal Artillery in World War II as a PT instructor in South Africa and India. It is believed his passion for acting came from his time in the army as a sports and entertainment officer; one of his duties was to organise shows for the troops. He became an actor at the relatively old age of 57, after retiring from the National Westminster Bank after more than 40 years' service. Unlike his TV character, forever replenishing his mariner's pipe, Merryfield never smoked, was teetotal and a fitness fanatic – sticking to a strict regime of swimming, press-ups and sit-ups. In 1996 he released his autobiography *During the War and other Encounters.* Sadly, Merryfield died, aged 78, in June 1999, as a result of a brain tumour. He was survived by Iris, his wife of 57 years.

Television

TRIGGERISMS

Over the years, Trigger didn't get that many lines in *Only Fools &
Horses*, but when he did they usually brought the house down... like
the time he took Del to the 24-hour waste disposal depot to get rid
of all the rubbish from Grandad's old allotment – only to find out
it was closed! When a furious Del says, "I thought you said it was
open 24 hours a day?" Trig responds, "Yeah... but not at night!" Then
there's the tale of his ever-lasting broom: the same broom he had
when he started sweeping roads... but has had countless new heads
and handles. Or perhaps the time Roy Slater returns for the reunion
party and apologises to Trig for setting him up with stolen Green
Shield Stamps. Trig accepts the apology, but then Boycie reminds
him he got sent away to a young offenders' institute for 18 months
as a result. Trig says, "I know. But when I came out I got an electric
blanket and a radio with 'em!"

"I saw one of them old £5 notes the other day."
Trigger, after Del's advice to talk about money to impress women.

"I know a lot of people are born 'apenny short of a shilling
but in Trigger's case God added VAT!"
Del on Trigger

"I heard later, through friends, that she wanted to go with me."
*Trigger explains why his relationship with one of his
co-workers ended after she had suggested to him
spending a weekend in Henley-on-Thames.*

"He died a couple of years before I was born."
Trigger on his dad

"I thought we was having a chat."
Trigger, after Del tells Denzil he and Trigger are in conference.

"She's a typical woman. Lies about her age."
*Trigger explains why his sister told everyone she was 42,
when in truth she was actually 39!*

"I used to fancy her."
Trigger muddles up Agatha Christie with Julie Christie.

"You'd think he'd be taking things easy in his condition."
*Trigger talking about the conman Arnie who rips off Del and
the boys over the gold chains by pretending he's retired due
to ill health, when of course he's not ill at all.*

"Oh turn it up... Trigger couldn't organise a prayer in a mosque."
Boycie on Trigger

"No, not very big. High ceilings though."
*Trigger's response to Rodney's question as to whether Del,
Boycie, Denzil and Trig had big classes at secondary school.*

"It's like having a séance with Mr Bean."
Boycie on what it's like staying at Trigger's flat for the night.

"I couldn't read."
Trigger explains how he walked into a Mind your Head sign.

"I thought we were all gonna jump out and surprise someone."
*Trigger explains why he spent an hour standing
in the dark in the dance hall at the Nag's Head.*

BIOGRAPHY: ROGER LLOYD PACK

Roger Lloyd Pack was born on 8th February 1944 and is best
known for his role as Trigger (the character's real name is Colin
Ball) in *Only Fools & Horses*. However, he has also starred in several
other TV series and films, most notably as Barty Crouch Senior in
Harry Potter and the Goblet of Fire. He is well known for his role in
The Vicar of Dibley as Owen Newitt – a character not dissimilar to
Trigger. Born in London, Lloyd Pack began acting at an early age;
his father Charles was also an actor. He has married twice; and
while with his first wife, Sheila Ball, he had one daughter Emily
Lloyd who is also an actress. Lloyd Pack's hobbies include snooker,
yoga and playing the piano.

FAMOUS FACES

Another of John Sullivan's traits was to have the boys mention famous faces in their jokes. Here are just a selection of a few of those who were referred to in the script – and a brief explanation as to why:

Sidney Poitier: Actor whose name Grandad cannot pronounce and he also muddles him up with the similar-looking actor Harry Belafonte in the opening episode 'Big Brother'.

Steve Bilko: Famous anti-apartheid campaigner, who adorned many a t-shirt of the "spoon-fed student type", according to Del Boy.

Genghis Khan: Del claims that if it came to a scrap over a torn fiver, Rodney and his student friends could make "Genghis Khan look like a pacifist". Khan was a Mongolian warlord from the 13th century.

Bamber Gascoigne: Del tells Rodney, "Two GCEs and you think you're Bamber Gascoigne's vest!" Whether he actually wore a vest is unconfirmed, but Eton-educated Gascoigne was the host of the BBC's high-brow quiz show *University Challenge*.

The Hollies: A music band who were the reason why many teen marriages broke up in the 1960s and 1970s – according to Del Boy because the husband wasn't a fan and the wife was!

Bertie Smalls: When Rodney dates Sandra, the policewoman, he refers to the infamous supergrass who gave evidence against the Krays, saying taking a bird to the pictures hardly makes him Bertie Smalls.

Freddie Laker: A famous entrepreneur who formed Laker Airways in the 1960s; Del says he wants to use Trotters' Ethnic Tours to become the Freddie Laker of the highways in 'A Slow Bus to Chingford'. Ironically, few months after this show aired Laker Airways went bust!

Arthur Negus: Rodney refers to antiques dealer Miranda Davenport as "Arthur Negus's youngest". Negus was an antiques expert who appeared on the BBC show *Antiques Roadshow*.

Bobby Crush: When Rodney appears in 'Watching the Girls go by' wearing a rather leery suit, bought from Paddy the Greek, Del Boy jokes, "I keep getting this yearning to put my Bobby Crush LP on!" Crush was an English pianist who presented the ITV gameshow *Sounds Like Music* – and had a tendency to wear similar suits to the one Rodney wore!

John Barnes: In 'The Class of '62' Rodney tells Del Boy that being stitched up by Raquel's estranged husband, former copper Roy Slater, must be like being "hit by a John Barnes' free-kick". Barnes was the Liverpool and England footballer who had a pretty powerful shot on him – particularly from free-kicks.

Diego Maradona: Del claims his new Capri Ghia handles like Maradona – the Argentinian footballer who infamously helped knock England out of the 1986 World Cup by punching the ball past Peter Shilton in the quarter-final.

Jive Bunny: Rodney says that Del sounds like Jive Bunny, because he keeps repeating himself. Jive Bunny and the Mastermixers were an 80s novelty pop music act (only the third band to have their first three releases go to number one on the UK singles chart) although their songs were of a distinctive repetitive nature.

Bros: The 1980s pop group Bros pop up in more than one episode. They get a mention when Del's trying to sell girls' dolls when he claims they're so realistic that they laugh, cry and, when they reach their teens, break out in acne and want to go to a Bros concert! While in 'The Unlucky Winner is...' Rodney, having been conscripted into the Groovy Gang, is stalked by Trudy, who viewers learn is a huge fan of the boy-band. The group – who were extremely popular with teenage girls in the 1980s – consisted of twin brothers Matt Goss and Luke Goss (giving the name Bros – short for brother) along with Craig Logan.

Dr Scholl: When Raquel tells Del Boy that the blame for AIDS lies firmly at the feet of mankind, Del tells her that if feet were the problem then Dr Scholl could have found a cure. William Scholl was a podiatrist from the early 20th century, who formed the Scholl foot care brand.

MORE FRENCH PHRASES

Répondez s'il vous plaut
Appellation Bordeaux controlée
Très bien ensemble
Crème de la menthe
Jeux sans frontières
Toujours la politesse, tourjours
Mon dieu
A la mode
Ordre du jour
Raise de chassie
Entende
Mon dieu
La bon vie!
Petit Suisse
Oeuf sur le plat
Ménage à trois
Marque de Fabrique
Potage bon femme!
Sienne va plus
Chamboussiz nouvelle
Revenons a nos moutons
Je nais sais pa poqua
A La Bruchette
Au contraire
Fromage Frais

WHO IS THE TALLYMAN?

In 'No Greater Love' Irene Mackay asks Rodney if he's the tallyman, which is a term from yesteryear. A tallyman is someone who sells goods, usually door-to-door, on an instalment plan... which is in fact exactly what Rodney ended up doing, selling Irene some clothes and letting her pay "on the weekly". In the 1970s and 1980s tallymen were quite popular, particularly on housing estates and in the poorer areas across the country, but in time have been replaced by big brand catalogues, which operate on the same principle.

MISTAKES

It's difficult for any scriptwriter not to make mistakes, and there are a few that eagle-eyed fans have spotted over the years in episodes of *Only Fools & Horses*. Del's actual age is one source of debate amongst fans, but then of course he could be fibbing. The *Only Fools & Horses* Appreciation Society's website (www.ofah.net) has an excellent episode guide which includes mistakes. In 'Mother Nature's Son', Del and Rodney are looking around Myles' organic farm food shop when Del notices the range of bottled water on sale. He is stunned that they actually bottle water and sell it, but he shouldn't be because he had previously poured Roy Slater a glass of it in 'Class of '62'. He stops Roy going into the kitchen (where Raquel's hiding) to get a glass of water and instead tells him to have a glass of "this trendy water" and pours him a glass from a Perrier bottle! In 'Fatal Extraction', while the natives are rioting, Albert says he won't go to the window because a brick might come through it; Rodney says they're on the 12th floor... However at the end of 'A Royal Flush', when Del and Rodney argue on the landing, the lift sign says it is the 13th floor!

NIGHTCLUBS & CASINOS

The Down by the Riverside Club
The Monte Carlo Club
The One Eleven Club
The 121 Club

BIOGRAPHY: JOHN CHALLIS

Motor-mouth car dealer Boycie is played by John Challis (who also stars as Boycie in the BBC's spin-off series *The Green Green Grass*). Challis, who appeared in the first series of *Only Fools & Horses*, was born on 16th August 1942 in Bristol. He began his acting career in 1964 and appeared in *Dixon of Dock Green*, *The Sweeney* and *Z Cars* before landing the role of Boycie. He has also appeared in *Coronation Street*, *The Bill*, and *Doctor Who*. In 2006 he presented UKTV Gold's countdown of *Only Fools & Horses'* top 40 moments.

ONLY FOOLS SOUNDTRACK

As time passed, music played a more integral part in *Only Fools & Horses*. From series six, much of the music is heard in the background, often in the pub, when presumably the Nag's Head also fitted a juke box! A number of well-known and some more obscure artists have featured over the years, and in 2002 the BBC released *Only Fools & Horses* the album – which includes 41 tracks used in the show over the years. The opening track is Simply Red's 'Holding Back The Years', which is used as Rodney's wedding draws to a close and viewers are left wondering if it's the end of *Only Fools & Horses*. The complete list of tracks (except opening and end-credit music which are listed in the next item) is:

Go West Young Man

Ain't No Stopping Us Now.. Enigma

Cash and Curry

Money... Pink Floyd

A Slow Bus to Chingford

Layback .... Rock Spectrum

Christmas Crackers

Three Times A Lady .... Brotherhood of Man
Daddy's Home..Cliff Richard
Shakin' All Over The World..Cliff Richard
Wordy Rappinghood...Tom Tom Club
Christmas Wrapping... The Waitresses
Bright Eyes .... Brotherhood of Man

It Never Rains...

In The Summertime .... Mungo Jerry

Diamonds Are For Heather

Zoom .... Fat Larry's Band

Healthy Competition

Theme from Jaws...John Williams

Wanted

Funky Moog..Disco Happening

Who's a Pretty Boy?

High Fly..Contemporary Orchestra

Thicker Than Water

Music from Sleepless Nights ....

It's Only Rock and Roll

Diane .... The Bachelors
Toot the Shoot.. Shakatak
Drivin' Hard, Boys Will Be Boys .... performed by Daniel Peacock
....written by John Sullivan

From Prussia With Love

I Didn't Mean To Turn You On..................................... Robert Palmer
Lady In Red..Chris De Burgh

Tea for Three

I Who Have Nothing.. Joan Baxter

Video Nasty

West End Girls... The Pet Shop Boys
Red Sky...Status Quo
Avalon..Brian Ferry and Roxy Music

A Royal Flush

Ask... The Smiths
Sometimes ....Erasure
Extracts from Bizet's Carmen...............................The Kent Orchestra
Music for the Royal Fireworks..G F Handel

The Frog's Legacy

Never Gonna Give You Up.. Rick Astley
FLM ....Mel and Kim
Faith..George Michael
Wake Me Up Before You Go ....Wham

So Macho ....Sinitta
Toy Boy...Sinitta
Smoke Gets In Your Eyes ....Brian Ferry

Dates

Burning Bridges ....Status Quo
Nothing Can Come Between Us................................Sade
Clean Heart...Sade
Haunt Me..Sade
Smokey Blues ....Aswad
Sad Song... The Christians

Yuppy Love

Love Goes Up and Down...................................Errol Brown
Enchanted Lady... The Passadenas
Lady In Red...Chris De Burgh

Danger UXD

Come Out To Play.. UB40
Stop.. Erasure Danger
Tribute (Right On)... The Passadenas
Fisherman's Blues ....The Waterboys
Is You Is Or Is You Isn't My Baby ....Joe Jackson
Jack You're Dead..Joe Jackson

Chain Gang

My One Temptation ....Mica Paris
Sweet Little Mystery....................................... Wet Wet Wet

The Unlucky Winner is...

That Ole Devil Called Love................................Alison Moyet
Why Does Love Got To Be So Sad......................Buckwheat Zydeco
Strange Kind Of Love................................. Love and Money
Love Train ....Holly Johnson
Lucy ....Habit
Hold Me In Your Arms .... Rick Astley
Birdie Song...The Tweets
Y Viva Espagna ....Sylvia

Sickness and Wealth

Where Is Your Love?..Gail Ann Dorsey
I Don't Want A Lover..Texas
Fine Time ....Yazz
Big Area...Then Jerico
It's Only Love...Simply Red

Little Problems

Only Want To Be With You..Sam Fox
Tender Hands...Chris De Burgh
Love Follows ....Steven Dante
Tracie .... Level 42
Looking For Linda..Hue and Cry
Bring Me Some Water..Melissa Etheridge
Buffalo Stance..Neneh Cherry
Something's Got Hold Of My Heart Marc Almond and Gene Pitney
Where Is The Love ....Mica Paris and Will Downing
Holding Back The Years..Simply Red

The Jolly Boys' Outing

Night Nurse..Gregory Isaacs
Now That We've Found Love..Third World
Over You..Roxy Music
Everybody Wants To Rule The World .... Tears For Fears
Help ....Bananarama
2.4.6.8. Motorway ....Tom Robinson Band
This Changing Light..Deacon Blue
Turn It Up ....Simply Red
Everybody's Talkin ....Nilsson
Just The Way You Are ....Lee Gibson
I May Be Wrong .... Alf Bigden, Ronnie Price, Dave Richmond
Sunshine of My Life .... Alf Bigden, Ronnie Price, Dave Richmond

Rodney Come Home

Reckless Man, Born To Be King ....Magnum
Let Me Be ....Fergal Sharkey
True..Spandau Ballet
Fascinating Rhythm ....Bassomatic

Don't Be A Fool ....Loose Ends
This Is The Right Time .... Lisa Stansfield
Rebel Yell ....Billy Idol
Did I Happen To Mention ....Julia Fordham
Your Lovely Face ....Julia Fordham
Somebody Who Loves You ....Joan Armatrading

The Sky's the Limit

Reckless Man, Born To Be King ....Magnum
Float On ....The Floaters
Opposites Attract .... Paula Abdul
Straight Up .... Paula Abdul

The Chance of a Lunchtime

All Around The World.. Lisa Stansfield
Promised Land .... Style Council
Do The Strand..Roxy Music
Love And Affection ....Joan Armatrading
Old Friends...Guitar Moods
Where Are You Baby ....Betty Boo
Eyes Without A Face .... Billy Idol
Masquerade .... Swing Out Sister

Stage Fright

Peace Through The World.. Maxi Priest
Love Is The Drug ....Roxy Music
Kick It In ....Simple Minds
Looking For Linda..Hue and Cry
Delilah .... Philip Pope
I'll Never Fall In Love Again... Philip Pope
Do You Know The Way To San Jose ....Tessa Peake-Jones
Crying... Tessa Peake-Jones and Philip Pope

The Class of '62

Never Enough .... The Cure
People.. Soul II Soul
Mighty Quinn .... Manfred Mann
All Around The World... Lisa Stansfield

Valentine's Day ....Betty Boo

He Ain't Heavy, He's My Uncle

Uncle Albert .... Paul and Linda McCartney

Three Men, a Woman and a Baby

Movies .... Hothouse Flowers
You Don't Have To Say You Love Me......................Dusty Springfield
Street Life ....Roxy Music
Nothing Compares To You ....Sinead O'Connor
Concerto in D Major ....Vivaldi

Miami Twice: The American Dream

Every Heartbeat .... Amy Grant
Hot Summer Salsa ....Jive Bunny and the Mastermixers
Englishman In New York ....Sting
White Wedding.. Billy Idol
Cold, Cold Heart.. Midge Ure
Let There Be Love.. Simple Minds

Miami Twice: Oh to be in England

Rockin' All Over The World ....Status Quo
Summer In The City ....The Gutter Brothers
Baby Baby.. Amy Grant
Hyperreal ....The Shamen
Killer ....Seal
Rush Rush .... Paula Abdul
Saltwater ....Julian Lennon
Born Free .... Vic Reeves

Mother Nature's Son

Merry Christmas Everybody .... Slade
Crocodile Rock.. Elton John
Who's Gonna Ride Your Wild Horses... U2
Could It Be Magic ....Take That
Santa Claus Is Coming To Town.......................................Bjorn Again
Money.. The Beatles

Fatal Extraction

Hands Up .... Right Said Fred
Step Into Christmas .... Elton John
Hope In A Hopeless World .... Paul Young
One Voice .... Barry Manilow
Whisper A Prayer .... Mica Paris
It's Alright .... East 17
Twist and Shout .... Chaka Demus and Pliers
Babe .... Take That
Stay (Faraway, So Close) U2
Mars, the Bringer of War .... Gustav Holst

Heroes and Villains

Sight For Sore Eyes .... M People
I Got You Babe .... UB40 with Chrissie Hynde
Knocking On Heaven's Door .... Children of Dunblane
Coming Home Now .... Boyzone
2 Become 1 .... The Spice Girls

Modern Men

Roll With It .... Oasis
Light Of My Life .... Louise
Love Me For A Reason .... Boyzone
Country House .... Blur

Time On Our Hands

Take Me Into Your Heart Again .... Vince Hill
Together .... Boyzone
Under The Moon Of Love .... Shawaddywaddy
I Wonder Why .... Shawaddywaddy
Our House .... Crosby, Stills, Nash and Young

If They Could See Us Now...!

Livin' La Vida Loca .... Ricky Martin
Somethin' Stupid .... Robbie Williams and Nicole Kidman
Symphony no. 38 in D major .... Mozart
Never Had A Dream Come True .... S Club 7
Can't Get You Out Of My Head .... Kylie Minogue

Can't Get Enough Of Your Love Babe ....Barry White
Gold ....Spandau Ballet

Strangers on the Shore

Flowers In The Window ....Travis
Dancing In The Moonlight ....Toploader

Sleepless in Peckham

Shoulda Woulda Coulda ....Beverley Knight
Uptown Girl ....Westlife
I Want It That Way ....Backstreet Boys
Dancing In The Moonlight ....Toploader
Sing ....Travis

TITLE MUSIC

The original theme music, written by Ronnie Hazlehurst, was only used in the first series. It was a seventies-style TV theme tune, with no lyrics which was played by musicians specially hired in by the BBC, including Alf Bigden who later played drums in the band which played the music during the nightclub scene in 'The Jolly Boys' Outing'. It was recorded at Lime Grove studios, but axed after the first series in favour of the theme written and sung by John Sullivan; a theme which explained what the title meant, and the one which everyone associates with the show nowadays. "My version had been written for the first series, and I thought they'd use it, but for some reason Ray [Butt] decided to go with Ronnie's." The plan was that Chas & Dave would sing the opening and closing theme, and it was written with them in mind – but when it came to recording there was a slight snag. "They had a number one hit and became very busy," continued Sullivan. "That was a bit of a choker because if they'd done our theme that might have gone to number one too. I'd recorded it originally just to get the tune, so Ray said to me, 'You do it.' I wasn't keen and had to be persuaded with lager!" The outcome was the opening theme 'Only Fools & Horses' and the closing theme 'Hookie Street'. Chas & Dave's hit 'Margate' was used as the closing music for 'The Jolly Boys Outing'. 'Rodney Come Home' played out to 'Somebody Who Loves You'; while 'Time On Our Hands' had the closing music 'Walking Into The Sunset'.

THE EPISODE GUIDES
SERIES 1-7 & SPECIALS

BIG BROTHER

Tuesday 8th September 1981 (8.30pm)   *30 minutes*
New characters: Del, Rodney, Grandad, Trigger.
In the opening episode, in which we meet Del, Rodney and Grandad, we also meet Trigger, from whom the boys buy some hookie briefcases. Del thinks they're onto a winner; Rodney's not convinced and the two brothers argue and Rodney disappears on one of his misguided attempts to prove himself. He returns (having done nothing of the sort) and discovers he was right all along and Del was wrong to buy the briefcases in the first place: the combinations to open the cases are locked inside!

GO WEST YOUNG MAN

Tuesday 15th September 1981 (8.30pm)   *30 minutes*
New character: Boycie
Del decides Trotters' Independent Traders' future lies in the second-hand car trade and starts out in a small way, by buying an old banger from Boycie (he gets a good price in return for storing Boycie's E-type Jag, which is a present for his bit on the side). Del then flogs the banger on to an unsuspecting Aussie punter for a decent profit – but after a night out up West to celebrate the deal, Del and Rodney meet up with the buyer for a second time... after the dodgy brakes on the banger cause him to crash into the back of the Jag... which Del has borrowed (without permission). Oh dear!

CASH AND CURRY

Tuesday 22nd September 1981 (8.30pm)   *30 minutes*
Del meets a new contact called Vimal Malik at the Chamber of Trade dinner dance – but as the pair are leaving, along with Rodney who has come to pick them up, Malik is hijacked by Mr Rahm. Del takes out Rahm's bodyguard, but Rodney and Malik drive off without him, meaning Del ends up going for a curry and a chat with Rahm. He learns that Rahm is apparently trying to buy back a statue from Malik. Del plots a con trick, based on the fact that the Indians' belief in the caste system does not allow the two Indian men to negotiate direct. The trick backfires as it's actually Del who gets conned for two grand!

THE SECOND TIME AROUND

Tuesday 29th September 1981 (8.30pm)   *30 minutes*

Del bumps into old-flame Pauline: single and back in Peckham after her two previous husbands have died. She is soon back with Del and living in the flat – but Rodney's suspicious. When Trigger phones Del to tell him that Pauline's two previous husbands died in suspicious circumstances, the Trotters do a runner and Del leaves Pauline a note telling her the engagement is off. When they return to the flat Rodney admits he put Trigger up to the call. Del doesn't mind, but he isn't happy that Pauline has rung the Australian talking clock and left the phone off the hook.

A SLOW BUS TO CHINGFORD

Tuesday 6th October 1981 (8.30pm)   *30 minutes*

Del comes up with Trotters' Ethnic Tours and gets the free hire of a bus, in return for Rodney acting as nightwatchman at the bus depot. However, the tours don't take off, with not one punter showing up in two days... although Del later discovers it might have something to do with Grandad not bothering to deliver the leaflets advertising the tours and throwing them down the rubbish chute.

THE RUSSIANS ARE COMING

Tuesday 13th October 1981 (8.30pm)   *30 minutes*

After Del buys a load of lead, Rodney discovers it's actually a nuclear fall-out shelter. So the brothers have a trial weekend testing it out... the only trouble is living in a flat they've got nowhere to put it and as the episode ends it shows the shelter on the top of Nelson Mandela House.

CHRISTMAS CRACKERS

Monday 28th December 1981 (9.55pm)   *30 minutes*

Grandad cooks Christmas lunch... badly and then just as Del's telling Rodney they're staying in with Grandad to keep him company, Grandad announces he's off out with the rest of the old folks on the estate. Del and Rodney end up in the Monte Carlo Club dancing the night away.

THE LONG LEGS OF THE LAW

Thursday 21st October 1982 (8.30pm)   *30 minutes*
New character: Sid
Much to Del's disgust Rodney takes WPC Sandra to the pictures, and brings her back to the flat, where she recognises lots of stolen items in the lounge. She tells Rodney she'll be round the next day with a warrant... meaning the Trotters have to spring clean their flat.

ASHES TO ASHES

Thursday 28th October 1982 (8.30pm)   *30 minutes*
Trigger's nan dies and Del clears his flat for him. He ends up with two valuable urns, one containing the ashes of Trig's grandad. As Del attempts to dispose of the ashes in a suitable fashion, the urn is sucked into a roadsweeper. Del talks his way out of any problems with Trigg, but then discovers his nan was married twice... and another urn

A LOSING STREAK

Thursday 4th November 1982 (8.30pm)   *30 minutes*
Superb episode which sees Del on a losing streak playing poker with Boycie and Trigger. Clean broke, Del has to turn to the emergency fund of £500 his mum left only for a life-and-death situation. In a no limits game (in which Del discovers Boycie's been cheating all along) it looks like Del's lost everything on a hand of two pairs, as Boycie reveals four kings. Until Del reveals a pair of aces and "another pair of aces".

NO GREATER LOVE

Thursday 11th November 1982 (8.30pm)   *30 minutes*
Rodney is selling door-to-door when he meets Irene Mackay, a 40-year-old wife of a convict. Rodney starts dating her, but soon learns her husband Tommy is due out of prison. He tells Del about the problem, who in turn asks Irene to dump Rodney. A chance meeting with Irene's son Marcus in the pub sees Rodney learn what Del's done... but then Tommy mistakes Del for Rodney. Feeling guilty, Del takes the beating so Rodney can restart his romance with Irene... only to discover Rodney's met someone else!

THE YELLOW PERIL

Thursday 18th November 1982 (8.30pm)   *30 minutes*
Del has some hookie paint from Trigger, so tricks Chinese takeaway owner Mr Chin into believing he is due a visit from the health inspector and therefore must paint his kitchen. Rodney and Grandad are lumbered with the job, while Del's off doing "this and that". When Trigger visits with more paint Rodney is disgusted to learn that the paint is stolen, but Del also discovers the paint is luminous. Mr Chin is placated when Del tells him it's energy saving paint, but in the final scene he shows Rodney what he's been up to: painting their mother's grave with the same paint!

IT NEVER RAINS

Thursday 25th November 1982 (8.30pm)   *30 minutes*
Del Boy tricks Alex the travel agent into a marketing promotion of offering a holiday for next to nothing... and it's no surprise that Del snaps up the offer and the family are off to Spain! Things go wrong when Grandad's arrested and in prison he confesses to the boys that he was deported from Spain for gun running during the war... Del bribes the prison guard with a fistful of notes, and then learns Grandad was only nicked for jaywalking and about to be released regardless of the bung!

A TOUCH OF GLASS

Thursday 2nd December 1982 (8.30pm)   *30 minutes*
The famous chandelier episode in which Del wins the contract to clean and restore two cut-glass chandeliers at Lord Ridgemere's stately home. The only trouble is when they start work on one chandelier, Grandad's working on another... with devastating consequences.

CHRISTMAS CRACKERS

Thursday 30th December 1982 (7.55pm)   *30 minutes*
Del is down on his luck, until he meets Heather at a Spanish night at the Nag's Head and is smitten by the single mum in this Christmas special. He decides to propose, but his plans are left in tatters when Heather tells him she's getting back with her son Darren's dad.

HOMESICK

Thursday 10th November 1983 (8.30pm)   *30 minutes*
Del and a supposedly-sick Grandad trick Rodney into becoming chairman of the tenants' association to get clearance for a move to a new council bungalow. Grandad pretends to be ill, and also tricks Miss MacKenzie from the council... until she pops back to the flat to take Del up on his offer to take her out and discovers Grandad's made an amazing recovery!

HEALTHY COMPETITION

Thursday 17th November 1983 (8.30pm)   *30 minutes*
New character: Mickey Pearce
Rodney dissolves his partnership with Del to go it alone with Mickey Pearce. The pair get off to a bad start as Del tricks them into buying some old lawnmower engines from him... and Rodney fails miserably, largely because Pearce does a runner with the rest of the money. Before long he's back in partnership with Del, but not before he's made another howler.

FRIDAY THE 14TH

Thursday 24th November 1983 (8.30pm)   *30 minutes*
A spot of weekend fishing at Boycie's cottage in Cornwall is disrupted after a con escapes from the nearby mental institute. The chief of security calls at the cottage, and while he's there Del knocks out a man lurking outside. The chief confirms it's the escapee; Rodney and Grandad take him to the police... where they learn it's really the local gamekeeper and the nutter is at the cottage with Del, about to play an imaginary game of snooker.

YESTERDAY NEVER COMES

Thursday 1st December 1983 (8.30pm)   *30 minutes*
Del advertises a supposed Queen Anne cabinet for sale and a Chelsea antiques dealer is interested. When she calls it looks as if she's wasted her time, until she spots a painting on the wall. Tricking Del into believing she fancies him, she cons him into giving her the painting "to hang in her bedroom". Of course she wants to sell it, but Del then tells her he's been trying to "get shot of it" as it was nicked.

MAY THE FORCE BE WITH YOU

Thursday 8th December 1983 (8.30pm)   *30 minutes*
New character: Roy Slater
Del's old school mate Roy Slater – now detective inspector – is looking for a hookie microwave oven. Rodney unwittingly takes him to Del, and facing the choice between a stretch or telling Slater who nicked it Del opts for the latter – but only on the proviso he first has immunity from prosecution. Del has the last laugh telling Slater he nicked it himself!

WANTED

Thursday 15th December 1983 (8.30pm)   *30 minutes*
Blossom, the local nutter, wrongly accuses Rodney of rape on the way back from the pub, after he stops her from falling over! By the morning Del has convinced Rodney that vigilante mobs are roaming the streets looking for the 'Peckham Pouncer'. It's all a wind up and Rodney, falling for it, goes on the run, before turning up in the water-tank room in the flats.

WHO'S A PRETTY BOY?

Thursday 22nd December 1983 (8.30pm)   *30 minutes*
New characters: Denzil and Mike Fisher
Del lands a job decorating Denzil and Corinne's living room, by undercutting Irishman Brendon. Del, Rodney and Grandad ignore instructions to stay out of the kitchen and let the kettle boil dry. They think the steam's killed Corinne's canary – replacing it with a £45 bird from the pet shop – but learn later that the canary was already dead!

THICKER THAN WATER

Sunday 25th December 1983 (9.35pm)   *30 minutes*
Del and Rodney's father is back in Peckham for Christmas, and quickly causes problems by casting doubts over whether Del is actually his son (he does this by doctoring Del and Rodney's blood test results). He also tells the boys he has a terminal illness, but it's all a lie to worm his way back into the flat. Del Boy sends him packing – albeit with a handful of notes to tide him over.

HAPPY RETURNS

Thursday 21st February 1985 (8.00pm)   *30 minutes*
Rodney is dating Debby – a cracking-looking bird who works in the
local newsagents, and is coming up to her 18th birthday – but trouble
is on the horizon when it turns out Del Boy had been dating her mum
June some eighteen-and-a-half years previously, leading him to believe
he's Debby's father. After telling Rodney to stay away from her, he plucks
up the courage to tell June that he's worked things out as to why she
left him – but it turns out Del's got it wrong and it's his late best friend
Albie Littlewood who was the father! However, it's too late for Rodney
to rekindle his romance with Debby, as Mickey Pearce has already stepped
in to date her!

STRAINED RELATIONS

Thursday 28th February 1985 (8.00pm)   *30 minutes*
New character: Uncle Albert
Grandad's funeral. A brilliantly written and emotional episode which
sees the brothers lay their late grandfather to rest. It also sees the arrival
of Uncle Albert, Grandad's brother, who is left behind at the funeral
by Cousin Stan and wife Jean (who also hitch up the caravan and do a
runner to avoid being lumbered with Albert the following morning).
After failing to secure a bed at the Seamen's Mission and facing the
prospect of homelessness, the old man of the seas ends up moving in
with Del and Rodney at Nelson Mandela House.

HOLE IN ONE

Thursday 7th March 1985 (8.00pm)   *30 minutes*
Albert falls down the cellar at the Nag's Head and Del Boy hires
Solly Attwell, the local solicitor who's dodgier than the criminals he
represents, to sue the brewery for compensation. After turning down
an offer of two grand, the case goes to court, where the council for the
defence uncovers the fact that Albert has pulled this trick several times
before! Del is told off by the judge and the case is thrown out – but
Albert tells the brothers he only wanted to get the money to pay for
Grandad's headstone.

IT'S ONLY ROCK AND ROLL

Thursday 14th March 1985 (8.00pm)　　　　　　　　*30 minutes*
Rodney joins a pop group – described by Del as a "bunch of wallies" – but after Del tricks them into playing a St Patrick's Night do at the Shamrock Club, for a £300 earner, Rodney leaves the band. It's not a problem, until Rodney sees his former band in the charts and performing on the BBC's *Top of the Pops*.

SLEEPING DOGS LIE

Thursday 21st March 1985 (8.00pm)　　　　　　　　*30 minutes*
New character: Marlene
Del dog sits for Boycie and Marlene while they're away, but Duke the dog falls ill. A visit to the vets fails to discover what's wrong, although the vet fears it may be salmonella poisoning from a joint of pork – which Albert has also eaten. Albert's admitted to hospital, but it's discovered Rodney has mixed up his uncle's sleeping pills with Duke's vitamins!

WATCHING THE GIRLS GO BY

Thursday 28th March 1985 (8.00pm)　　　　　　　　*30 minutes*
Rodney is ribbed by Mickey Pearce about a lack of offers from girls, so he bets him "fifty" that he'll bring a bird to the Nag's Head party later that week. Del buys the bet off Rodney and attempts to line him up with a date: eventually succeeding with Yvonne the stripper... Rodney is mortified when she goes through her routine, to the delight of everyone in the pub; Del is mortified when he learns the "fifty" is actually 50 pence.

AS ONE DOOR CLOSES

Thursday 4th April 1985 (8.00pm)　　　　　　　　*30 minutes*
Del borrows Denzil's redundancy money to cut a deal and make some dosh on some hookie louvre doors – but having bought the doors, his buyer changes his mind. Denzil and his brothers come looking for the cash Del's promised and the Trotters have to scarper and find sanctuary in the park – where Rodney spots a rare butterfly worth three grand. After catching it, Del's cash-flow problem is solved... or so it seems!

FROM PRUSSIA WITH LOVE

Sunday 31st August 1986 (8.35pm)   *30 minutes*

Rodney comes to the aid of pregnant German au pair Anna. He meets her in the Nag's Head and discovers she's been thrown out by her host family, after getting in the family way, and is left with an unwanted pregnancy and nowhere to stay. Del tries to assist the poor girl and lines up a deal to sell her unborn child to Boycie and Marlene! But things hit a snag when the baby arrives and Anna decides against flogging her child... what's more Boycie goes cold on the deal after a little unexpected surprise.

THE MIRACLE OF PECKHAM

Sunday 7th September 1986 (8.35pm)   *30 minutes*

Del disappears to confession one morning, and on his way out of the church notices the Virgin Mary statue is crying. He sells the story to media organisations worldwide and the £185,000 is enough to save the local hospice from closure. It's only after all the news crews have left that it is discovered that the miracle is actually rain coming through the leaking church roof, due to the lead being stolen... and that Del was confessing to buying the stolen lead, albeit unaware it was from the roof of the church.

THE LONGEST NIGHT

Sunday 14th September 1986 (8.35pm)   *30 minutes*

Del, Rodney and Albert are accused of shoplifting, after losing their receipt for their groceries at the local supermarket. Then a real shoplifter is brought into the office and holds up the manager at gunpoint and demands that he open the safe. It's impossible as the safe is on a timelock and won't open until the morning, so the Trotters – and the manager and head of security – are trapped for the night. Eventually the gunman, young Lennox, admits it's all a set-up and he was talked into it by the supermarket boss and security man, who are both in on it. Del threatens to go to the law, but a compromise is reached when the manager agrees to give Lennox a job... and ensure Del becomes the supermarket's one millionth customer with a prize of £1000!

TEA FOR THREE

Sunday 21st September 1986 (8.35pm)   *30 minutes*

Del and Rodney are both interested in Lisa, who's staying with her uncle Trigger. She comes to tea at the flat, but before she arrives Del leaves Rodney sleeping under the home sunbed... and even turns up the timer to make sure he burns. Rodney is left red-faced, but gets his own back by arranging for Del to have a go at hang-gliding with some of Lisa's friends, when they drop her home to the south coast. Del's macho pride means he can't back out and with Rodney doing nothing to help him, Del ends up in the clouds, but soon comes back to earth with a bump!

VIDEO NASTY

Sunday 28th September 1986 (8.35pm)   *30 minutes*

Rodney is given a grant to make a community film (along with Mickey Pearce). Unbeknown to Rodney, Del gets Mickey, who's already in possession of the video camera, filming weddings at £50 a time – while Rodney's drawn the short straw of writing the script! The film script isn't as easy as Rodney thinks it'll be, even with his brother's help (Del suggests a film called "there's a rhino loose in the city") but that's only the beginning as his problems get even worse when Mickey uses the Trotters' flat to film a blue movie with interesting consequences.

WHO WANTS TO BE A MILLIONAIRE

Sunday 5th October 1986 (8.35pm)   *30 minutes*

Del's old pal from schooldays Jumbo Mills is back in town to complete an import-export deal with Boycie, to ship prestigious English cars to Australia. While he's back in Peckham he offers Del the opportunity to join him in his business venture down under as a partner in the venture – and bring Rodney along with him too. Del can't believe his luck (and Rodney's pretty pleased too, even if he will be cleaning cars to start with) but that's until the boys' visa application responses arrive back: Del's accepted, but Rodney gets rejected because of his conviction for smoking pot while at college. Del looks set to go on his own, and hand Trotters Independent Traders over to Rodney – until family ties trigger a last-minute change of mind.

YUPPY LOVE

Sunday 8th January 1989 (7.15pm)   *50 minutes*
New character: Cassandra

In the first of the 50-minute episodes a now yuppy Del Boy reveals that he's applied to buy the Trotters' flat from the local council – so he can sell it at a profit and buy a nice drum elsewhere. Rodney accuses him of being a snob, but after he meets Cassandra for the first time at evening school and then bumps into her again at the disco, the boot is on the other foot as he tells her he lives in the posh Kings Avenue. Del Boy also goes drinking in a wine bar with Trigger... and falls through the open bar.

DANGER UXD

Sunday 15th January 1989 (7.15pm)   *50 minutes*

Del buys some damaged dolls from Denzil – which don't officially exist, after he failed to return them to the factory, and then the factory went up in smoke. They turn out to be blow-up dolls of the adult variety, and unbeknown to Del have been on the local news as missing, because they're filled with an explosive gas. Del Boy tries to sell them to Dirty Barry, a local sex-shop owner. He fails and so decides he'll keep them until the market for such products picks up again – but Rodney finally learns about the gas and gives Del Boy the bad news just in time...

CHAIN GANG

Sunday 22nd January 1989 (7.15pm)   *50 minutes*

Del meets Arnie – a retired jewellery dealer, who despite suffering from heart trouble, still does a bit of business on the side. Del sets up a deal to buy 250 gold chains at a knock-down price; chains which Arnie had bought for a tough-guy client Maxi Stavros, who's now gone awol. Del puts together a consortium – himself, Boycie, Mike, Trigger, Albert and eventually Rodney – to buy the chains, but no sooner is the deal done, when Arnie learns from his wife Pat that Maxi's back on the scene wanting his gold. The consortium agree to let Arnie sell the chains on to Stavros, on their behalf, in order to keep his limbs intact. However, having agreed to meet Stavros, Arnie suffers a heart-attack... or so you think. It's all a con trick, but eventually Del and co catch up with Arnie.

THE UNLUCKY WINNER IS...

Sunday 29th January 1989 (7.15pm)   *50 minutes*

Del Boy's latest craze is competitions and he gets lucky winning a holiday to Spain, by entering one of Rodney's paintings. Oddly the holiday, courtesy of Megaflakes, is for three people, but it's only when they arrive that Del tells Rodney and Cassandra that the painting won in the under-14 category. Rodney has to pose as a 14-year-old, Del as his dad and Cassandra as his stepmother. Rodney is conscripted into the Groovy Gang and spends the week partaking in various children's activities – including skateboarding, cycling and break-dancing.

SICKNESS AND WEALTH

Sunday 5th February 1989 (7.15pm)   *50 minutes*

Del is suffering with a dodgy stomach, and Rodney and Albert want him to go to the doctors, but Del is more concerned with his latest business venture... a séance night at the Nag's Head, at which he'll charge punters to contact departed relatives. However, on the trial run, Del gets a message from his late mother to go and see the doctor: where, after giving the doctor the impression he's a picture of health, he is sent straight to hospital. Eventually, he's properly diagnosed and is on the mend, until Rodney gives him some surprise news...

LITTLE PROBLEMS

Sunday 12th February 1989 (7.15pm)   *50 minutes*
New characters: Alan and Pamela Parry

A cracking episode in which Rodney gets married to Cassandra, but before the wedding Del's got some more pressing problems... like a two-grand debt to the Driscoll brothers for 50 mobile phones he picked up from Mickey Pearce and Jevon. The Driscolls come looking for Del and warn him to pay up or else. Thankfully for Del, Boycie thinks they're chasing the money he owes Del for video recorders, and pays out the three grand he owes him. Problem solved? Not so, Del's also promised Rodney two grand as a deposit for his flat. Rodney thinks he's missed out, but Del takes the punishment from the Driscolls rather than let his brother down just before his big day.

THE SKY'S THE LIMIT

Sunday 30th December 1990 (7.15pm)   *50 minutes*

Boycie's dodgy satellite receiver gets nicked from his back garden, so he goes to Del Boy, telling him to buy it back, rather than report it to the police. Del buys what he thinks is the dish, but later discovers Boycie has his back. In the meantime Rodney is off to the airport to pick up Cassandra, but discovers the airport is in turmoil and Cassandra's flight has been re-routed to Manchester. The reason for the chaos is because the main satellite has been nicked from the end of the runway... and that's the one Del Boy has sitting on his balcony at Nelson Mandela House.

THE CHANCE OF A LUNCHTIME

Sunday 6th January 1991 (7.15pm)   *50 minutes*

Raquel has an audition for a part in the Shakespeare play *As You Like It*. While she's rehearsing at home with Del, Rodney's out with Cassandra and manages to patch things up with her, until she jumps to the wrong conclusion when she sees him trying to help Del's old-flame Trudy into the back of a taxi. When Alan calls the flat, Rodney gets the wrong end of the stick, and fearing the sack hands in his resignation. Alan accepts much to Del's disgust... Meanwhile, after her audition Raquel learns she's got the part, in what is a tour of inner-city schools, but tells Del she won't be taking it because she's pregnant.

STAGE FRIGHT

Sunday 13th January 1991 (7.15pm)   *50 minutes*

Del gets a call from his old 'mate' Eric from the Starlight Rooms who, having heard he is living with a singer, asks him if Raquel would provide a cabaret act for the nightclub. Del's reluctant – until Eric offers him £600 for providing an act for the night. He eventually talks Raquel into performing at the club, but only on the proviso that she has someone singing on stage with her, as her previous solo performances have been disasters. Del recruits Tony Angelino the singing dustman... with hilarious consequences.

THE CLASS OF '62

Sunday 20th January 1991 (7.15pm)   *50 minutes*

Del is invited to a school reunion at the Nag's Head – along with Boycie, Denzil and Trigger – but they're all in the dark as to who has organised the party... until Roy Slater – recently released from prison – turns up. He apologises to all those present for his previous misdemeanours against them and they accept and the night ends in a drinking session at Del's. When Raquel returns to the flat, she recognises Slater, asleep on the sofa, as her former husband with whom she's going through divorce proceedings; meaning Del has to come up with a way of persuading Roy to leave quietly without revealing the truth...

HE AIN'T HEAVY, HE'S MY UNCLE

Sunday 27th January 1991 (7.15pm)   *50 minutes*

There are a lot of muggings on the estate, and Albert is mugged on his way home from a domino tournament at the Nag's Head. Del Boy is fuming and vows to get even with the skinheads who have recently begun frequenting the pub, as he suspects them to be the muggers. Albert goes missing – after a bit of tough-love treatment from Del – and the boys spend the day looking for him around London. They eventually find him at Tobacco Road – where he grew up – and bring him back to the flat, where Knock Knock pops round and tells Del he and Albert had a fight... and that he wasn't mugged. The only trouble is that Del's already arranged to get even with the 'muggers'.

THREE MEN, A WOMAN AND A BABY

Sunday 3rd February 1991 (7.15pm)   *50 minutes*
New character: Damien

Raquel's on the verge of giving birth to her baby; Del's got a new range of wigs from his mate Mustapha; while Rodney finally gets back with Cassandra, after saving her from a 'rat' which is actually a dreadful clip-on ponytail, borrowed from Del's latest line in stock. Raquel goes into labour, and Rodney is summoned to the hospital to be present for the birth, where after plenty of pushing and screaming Del's first son Damien Trotter is born.

TO HULL AND BACK

Wednesday 25th December 1985 (7.30pm)　　　　　　*90 minutes*
Del, Rodney and Albert become international diamond couriers as part of Boycie and Abdul's smuggling racket. After Del and Rodney end up in Hull by mistake, the Trotters hire a boat to get them to and from Amsterdam. On arrival back home, bent copper Roy Slater supposedly busts the racket – but it's all for his own gain, until he is caught out by an undercover sting.

A ROYAL FLUSH

Thursday 25th December 1986 (7.05pm)　　　　　　*80 minutes*
Rodney meets Vicky – daughter of the Duke of Maylebury – and starts dating her, but thanks to Del's interference things don't go very well. A night at the opera ends in disaster and when Rodney is invited to a weekend shooting party at the Duke's estate, Del turns up unannounced and engineers an invite to dinner... where once again his helping hand is anything but.

THE FROG'S LEGACY

Friday 25th December 1987 (6.25pm)　　　　　　*60 minutes*
The Trotters are off to Hampshire for Trig's niece's wedding, where Del discovers he and Rodney are the heirs to a million quid's worth of gold bullion, left to their mum by her 'friend' Freddy the Frog. The only trouble is they don't know where it was buried. Rodney's work as a chief mourner leads the Trotters to the gold...

DATES

Sunday 25th December 1988 (5.05pm)　　　　　　*80 minutes*
New character: Raquel
After seeing Trigger out to lunch with a stunner, Del Boy signs up to the Technomatch agency, which arranged the date for Trigger. Del meets Raquel and things are going well until he finds out, in the worst possible way, that she's a stripper. Also, Rodney's playing the dating game too, and things don't go well for him either with barmaid Nervous Nerys.

THE JOLLY BOYS' OUTING

Monday 25th December 1989 (4.05pm)   *85 minutes*
The Trotters and co all head off to Margate for the jolly boys' outing, organised by Del. Things don't start well as Rodney's nicked for kicking a football at a policeman, and after a day at the fun fair and on the beach, things get worse when the coach blows up. The party have to stay the night in Margate, which isn't good news, until Del bumps into old flame Raquel.

RODNEY COME HOME

Tuesday 25th December 1990 (5.10pm)   *75 minutes*
Things aren't going well between Rodney and Cassandra and after another row, Rodney moves out of the flat for the third time in 18 months – but with Raquel now living at Nelson Mandela House (in Rodney's old room) things are a little cramped. Things get worse for Rodney as he takes some bad advice from Mickey Pearce, and Del fails in his attempts to get him back with Cassandra...

MIAMI TWICE: THE AMERICAN DREAM

Tuesday 24th December 1991 (7.30pm)   *50 minutes*
It's Damien's chrsitening and while at church Del's come up with an idea... Trotters' pre-blessed communion wine! Meanwhile Rodney gets a cheque from his former boss Alan and uses the money to splash out on a holiday to Miami for himself and Cassandra. The only trouble is that she can't go because of a work commitment and Del has to go instead!

MIAMI TWICE: OH TO BE IN ENGLAND

Wednesday 25th December 1991 (3.10pm)   *95 minutes*
Del and Rodney are holidaying in Miami, where they bump into the local mafia. Del is a dead ringer for mafia boss Don Ochetti – who's on trial and facing prison – so Del's set up by their 'hosts' for a public death meaning "in the eyes of America... no Don Ochetti" and no trial. Del survives a shooting and drowning attempt before he realises what's going on and he and Rodney leg it back to England.

MOTHER NATURE'S SON

Friday 25th December 1992 (6.55pm)   *65 minutes*
Raquel discovers that Del Boy has bought their flat from the council and isn't too happy about it, especially as the mortgage is two and a half times the rent... and they couldn't afford the rent! But after a visit to an organic farm shop, Del comes up with a plan to solve the Trotters' money problems by selling bottled water from the Peckham 'spring', recently discovered on Grandad's old allotment.

FATAL EXTRACTION

Saturday 25th December 1993 (6.05pm)   *85 minutes*
Del's late nights out drinking and gambling don't go down very well at home with Raquel and eventually she and Damien move out (and in with Rodney and Cassandra). On the rebound Del agrees to take out the receptionist at the dentist's surgery, where he's having his tooth out, but realising he's made a mistake doesn't go through with the date and instead makes it up with Raquel... but has he already made a terrible mistake?

HEROES AND VILLAINS

Wednesday 25th December 1996 (9.00pm)   *60 minutes*
Having had his home-improvement grant rejected and with Raquel away at her parents', Del's latest money-making scheme is for Rodney and him to win a fancy dress contest dressed as Batman and Robin. Unfortunately they arrive at the party to find the host died a few days earlier, (Del didn't get the message)... but the deadly duo later reap their reward, after catching a gang of muggers.

MODERN MEN

Friday 27th December 1996 (8.00pm)   *60 minutes*
Del Boy's reading a book 'Modern Man', which has him offering to have a vasectomy... With his usual financial worries, plus the added burden of Dr Singh chasing him for a refund on some dodgy paint, eventually he changes his mind and focuses on a new invention: Trotter Crash Turbans. The episode ends on a sad note as Cassandra loses her baby.

TIME ON OUR HANDS

Sunday 29th December 1996 (8.00pm)   *60 minutes*

Raquel's mum and dad, Audrey and James, come to dinner at Nelson Mandela House to meet Del and the family; and Albert manages to mix up the gravy and coffee. Raquel's dad James is back the following day to collect his car from Del's garage and spots the long-lost Lesser Watch in amongst the junk. It's auctioned for £6.2m and after years of trying the Trotters are finally millionaires!

IF THEY COULD SEE US NOW...!

Tuesday 25th December 2001   *71 minutes*

Having invested their new-found wealth in the Central American futures market, a market crash means the Trotters are now bust and facing a massive bill from the Inland Revenue. Facing eviction, Del goes on the gameshow *Goldrush* to try and win enough money to pay the taxman and save the family from homelessness. The episode also sees the funeral of Uncle Albert.

STRANGERS ON THE SHORE

Wednesday 25th December 2002   *75 minutes*

An invite for Albert to attend a naval reunion in France is accepted by Del and Rodney. The boys discover a little secret about Albert while abroad and Del has also arranged a duty free pick up for the Nag's Head on the way home... but what he didn't bargain for was 'Gary' the illegal immigrant who turns out to be the son of the millionaire owner of the beer and wine warehouse, who is also one of Boycie's new business contacts.

SLEEPLESS IN PECKHAM

Thursday 25th December 2003   *75 minutes*

After failing with *Goldrush* and beer importing, the Trotters are still facing eviction... until Del and Rodney learn that Albert's left them enough to see off the taxman, plus about another £100,000 on top. The last episode of the show also sees Rodney learn who his real father was... and sees the birth of Rodney and Cassandra's daughter, Joan.

CHRISTMAS TREES

Monday 27th December 1982 (8.05pm)   *8 minutes*

Trotters Independent Traders is doing a nice line in telescopic Christmas trees, the only trouble is they aren't selling very well in the market... in fact, as Del puts it, they're going down like Union Jacks in Buenos Aires. That is until he sends Rodney to the local church to give the vicar one for free. Del soon sells out his stock, by telling punters it's the only tree recommended by the Church of England.

LICENSED TO DRILL

1984 onwards   *27 minutes*

An educational episode, used to teach secondary school students about the benefits of North Sea oil. After reading a magazine and watching a programme on BBC2, Del is suddenly an expert on oil and thinks he's going to make his fortune from it – but he is conned into buying a non-existent oil rig for £400. The episode is significant for Grandad's last-ever appearance.

THE ROBIN FLIES AT DAWN

Saturday 1st December 1990   *15 minutes*

A special episode filmed and broadcast for British troops fighting in the Gulf War. The spoof message sees Del, "reporting from a secret location somewhere in southern England". He later accidentally reveals "it's High Wycombe". He tells the troops that he has a top-secret plan, involving three-wheeler tanks, and not to worry as he will look after their birds until they get back.

COMIC RELIEF SPECIAL

Friday 14th March 1997 (7.40pm)   *7 minutes*

Del and Rodney begin the special episode discussing possible holiday destinations; Del then reveals he is considering putting forward Damien for child modelling before Albert brings up Africa and the episode moves on to touch on the issues covered by Comic Relief and ends with a to-camera appeal for donations from viewers at home.

PECKHAM TRADERS' HANDBOOK
MANUSCRIPT SUBMISSION

PECKHAM TRADERS' HANDBOOK
MANUSCRIPT SUBMISSION

Over the following pages, you will
find useful business advice gleaned
from years of trading in the markets
and pubs, and on the streets, around
Peckham and South East London.

MONEY

Traders have their own monetary
terms, which the likes of Gordon
Gecko, Nigel Lawson and Norman Lamont
are unlikely to be familiar with.
It's important to learn the lingo
down Hookey Street or you could end
up losing out on a nice little earner
and instead find yourself done up like
a kipper – as Macbeth said to Hamlet
in a Midsummer Night's Dream.

Bangers (and mash)	Cash
Boracic (lint)	Skint
Holding (the folding)	Got money
Nelson (Eddies)	Readies
Score	£20
Pony	£25
Century	£100
Deuce in bunce	£200
Monkey	£500
Grand	£1000

TRADING

There is a very fine line between being a successful trader and not. Lots of people are achievers, but too many of them don't actually achieve anything. With this in mind it's always important to keep the long-term aim firmly in focus – such as being a millionaire within a year. An old Peckham fly pitcher once said: "You can go out in the morning with fifty pence in your pocket and come home skint." Equally you never know, you might pick up that bargain of a lifetime that eventually makes you a millionaire. Kidology is always an important tactic: like a game of poker, never reveal your hand.

CONTACTS

Build up your buying and selling contacts around the pubs, clubs and casinos, but always play it cool when buying and selling. Always remember if things get bad financially never let on to your contacts or competitors – as they'll be the first to flush you down the karzi. So maintain a yuppy profile; keep drinking in the wine bars and bistros to make everyone think all is well fiscally.

BUYING

Don't be put off by where things come
from (often that's where the bargains
lie): you can buy Albanian stereos,
'Italian' shirts from Malaya, Russian
VCRs, Fijian skiwear… it all shifts
eventually. Beware Romanian Riesling
and fads and fashions. Examples
of some really bad buys are: Bros
LPs, Charles and Di Wedding plates
and Free Nelson Mandela t-shirts.
And remember, never let on you're
interested in buying something –
otherwise the vendor will expect a
fair price. Always talk things down.
For example, tell them gold jewellery
is 9 carat if they say it's 18 carat.

SELLING

Completely the opposite to buying:
talk everything up – that 18 carat
jewellery becomes 27 carat – while
another good trick is to tell them
someone famous uses one – such as
Prince Charles or Nigel Mansell.
Another good marketing technique
is to give a demonstration on one
of the punters. For example if
you're selling something like a deep
penetration back massager, pull one
of the punters from the crowd who

appears to have back trouble – or better still get an elderly relative to pretend you've never met before in your life. Remember don't call each other by first name terms as it can put the punters right off!

AT THE AUCTION

The auction is always a good source of stock – from porcelain statues to fire damaged woks – but the newcomer should be careful of various rules and etiquette. Something as innocent as scratching your nose can be construed as a bid by the auctioneer. Another important rule at the auction – especially if you spot a little gold nugget in amongst the usual run-of-the mill stuff: don't let on to your competitors what it is you're keen to buy. If possible send them off on a tangent, by telling them to stay away from something completely different in the catalogue. For example, if you want the cut glass goblets, then play some mind games, double bluff your competitors and let them think you're after something completely different, like broken lawnmower engines. This can also prove an extra bonus, if you are selling the broken engines.

TAX ISSUES

If you're self-unemployed it may be much easier to keep things simple and cut down on the old paperwork. It might be easier not to pay income tax or National Insurance contributions and then even things out by not claiming dole money, social security or supplementary benefit. That way things balance out as the government aren't giving you nothing and you don't give the government nothing.

PARTNERSHIPS

These are usually best avoided – but they can be a very useful ruse to convince a little plonker they're a valued member of the team, when all you want them to do is all the dirty work and heavy lifting. These partnerships can be quite lopsided. For example it can be a combination of one guy's business acumen, contacts and money and the other guy's ability to drive a three-wheeled van... badly. A useful phrase to use from time to time, just to make them feel valued is something like: "It's everything split straight down the middle between you and me: that's 60:40."

PECKHAM & SOUTH LONDON PHRASEOLOGY

Choice phrases to help with the lingo:

Arras	Backside
Bandito	Gay man (bandit)
Brahma	Sort
Cosmic	Outstanding
Cushty	Excellent, okay
Dipstick	Plonker
Earner	a profitable deal
Enemy	Wife, missus
Gandhi's revenge	A dodgy stomach
Jacksie	Arras
Jaffa	Infertile, seedless
Karzi	Toilet
Kosher	Legitimate
Manor	Area you live/work
Mucker	Mate
Nitto	No
Noofter	Bandito
Pad	House
Potless	Brassic
Plonker	An idiot
Pukka	Great, perfect
Schtum	To keep quiet
Sort	An attractive bird
Stuk	A tricky situation
Triffic	Wonderful, super
Twonk	Plonker
Upper and a downer	Disagreement
Wally	Twonk
You can't whack it	You can't beat it

RHYMING SLANG

These phrases may also come in handy:

April (in Paris)	Arras, bum
Boracic (lint)	Skint
Dog (and bone)	Phone
Mutt (and Jeff)	Deaf
Ruby Murray	Curry
Stoke on Trent	Bent, gay
Taters (in the mould)	Cold

USEFUL PHONE NUMBERS TO INCLUDE:

Peckham (& Camberwell) Chamber of Trade: they hold a blinding dinner dance: a good place to meet contacts.

The One Eleven Club and The 121 Club: two casinos which are regular haunts for local businessmen in Peckham.

Alan Parry: He provides the best print in Peckham. Give him a bell if you need any printing done.

The Advanced Electronics, Research & Development Centre
~~Ron's Cash & Carry~~: Plenty of bargains (stock!) here, and they have a Queen's Award for Industry.

Transworld Express: Any time, any load, anywhere. The bestest couriers in the whole of Peckham and London.